Je mist meer dan je meemaak
helemaal niet erg.

— Martin Bril

For Oswald.

Don't Read This Book

Time Management for Creative People

Table of Contents

**Why Creative People
Need Time Management**

The ToDon'tList Method

Life:
Make a Plan

Work:
Create a Routine

Projects:
Leave Out Extras

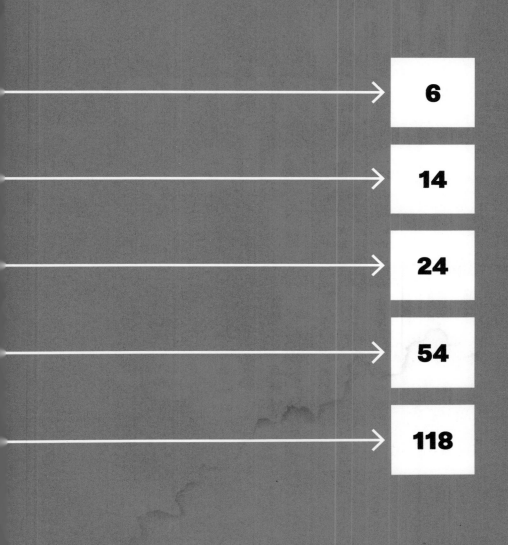

Why Creative People Need Time Management

A good artist has less time than ideas.

— Martin Kippenberger

'IDEA' DEVELOPMENT CENTRE

I am convinced that the execution is more important than having an idea. That's just the seed. Turning that into an entire tree is difficult and hard.

— Elon Musk

 EXECUTION TIME

Creative people have ideas. That's why we're called creatives. We look at the world through different eyes. We are inspired and continually come up with ideas. Everywhere. Day in, day out: Ping! A new idea pops up! We can't help it. And therein lies the crux of our problem. We have more ideas than time to execute them.

If you work on too many ideas at once, you run the great risk of all your ideas constantly being half-finished. Or arriving at an end result that delights nobody. There is simply not enough time to carry out all your ideas. Make sure you spend your time well.

Time management can help you to do so. Perhaps creativity and time management seem like contradictions. However, if you look at big names in the creative world, you will quickly see that these artists and designers work with fixed routines and sophisticated methods. They can do what they do, because they guard their time well. Their trick is: they do fewer different things in the time they have and leave out anything that isn't essential. They limit themselves to the core of their work.

Don't believe the productivity gurus

Thinking in terms of productivity stems from the time of the industrial revolution. The longer a machine runs during a day, the higher the productivity. Make the machines faster, smarter and more efficient, and the productivity increases exponentially.

Productivity gurus view people as machines of a sort: if they work longer hours every day, they are more productive. But people are not machines. People cannot constantly be productive. A machine can be switched on and left running. Humans don't work that way. Plus, a working day of 8 hours is not at all as efficient as it seems: working long hours does not equal more effective work.

Start-up Buffer also realised this and decided to no longer measure productivity in terms of time. Instead, the teams and employees were given clear objectives and domains within which they were given responsibility. This strategy also enabled them to remove an expensive management layer from the organization. Their motto: "How you do it is up to you, as long as you do it."

To do, or not to do; that's the question

So, in order to manage your time well, you don't have to plan everything at a detailed level. Instead, consider a bigger goal. Then make your choices based on that: What will you do and what won't you do?

These can be hard decisions to make. But read on and I promise: it will soon become easier.

Where Do Ideas Come From?

The evolution of ideas

Everything we see around us — except for nature — was once an idea someone had. Charles and Ray Eames may have designed iconic chairs, but the idea of the chair emerged when a distant ancestor found a rock and sat down on it. Every invention flows from previous ideas. Often ideas seamlessly merge from one into the other, but some feature as milestones in the evolution of ideas, like Henry Ford's idea to manufacture cars at a large scale. He did not invent the car itself. Nor did he invent the assembly line. But his idea to combine the two became a milestone in production history.

Everything is connected

Google would never have existed if Tim Berners-Lee had not invented the World Wide Web, which became the method for viewing the Internet (which was already in place) through personal computers. The Internet itself emerged from a network of telephone lines between various universities. Telephone lines, in turn, emerged from telegraph machines.

Innovation is serendipity, so you don't know what people will make.

— Tim Berners-Lee

From one idea grows another, often without us being able to anticipate it. That's because ideas don't function along linear lines, but come together through all sorts of twists and turns: something that philosopher Gilles Deleuze calls a Rhizome. A Rhizome is a root that grows and worms its way into everything. It is symbolic for how connotations and ideas work: You are standing at a crossing with a random number of directions. You turn into the road that feels like it suits you best. Only in retrospect can you see what the choices you've made were good for.

Time Management for Creative People is therefore not an hour-by-hour planning method, but a way to help you decide which route you wish to take, even if your goal is not entirely clear yet. In brief: you execute some quick tests to decide which road suits you best. Sounds vague to you? No worries, I will come back to this in a minute.

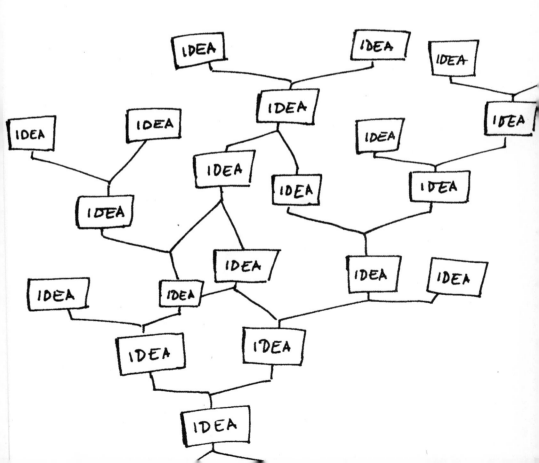

The To-Do List

A very short history of the to-do list

When bartering became impractical (not everyone needed a goat), tokens were used. But an entire urn filled with tokens soon became quite unhandy, too. That's how the first lists em-erged: so that people wouldn't have to spend time counting tokens and dragging them around. Or keep track of what others still owed them. This is ultimately also why writing was invented.

The list is the origin of culture. Wherever you look in cultural history, you will find lists.

— Umberto Eco

Organize your ideas

Ideas keep popping up in our minds, one after the other. We often continue to walk around with all of these ideas in our heads. They buzz around in there like restless mosquitoes. All those loose fragments take up incredible amounts of brain space, more particularly in the part that is known as your Conscious Brain — that part of your brain that receives infor-mation, but also contains the part with which you focus on ac-tivities: your working memory. You also have an Unconscious Brain, which offers lots of space for storing your ideas and information that you don't immediately need. It's a hard disk of sorts. If you store your ideas there, you conveniently reduce the 'restless mosquitoes' in your Conscious Brain.

How to make this happen? Write your ideas down. Once an idea or 'to-do' has made its way onto a list, we are free to forget about it, which silences the 'buzzing mosquitoes' in the active part of our brains. That part of the brain then becomes available again for focused use. For the religious readers among you: even God had a to-do list of seven points when he created the Earth.

Unfinished business

Of course, to-do lists are not perfect either: they can become endless. You can add as many to-dos as you wish. With as its major danger that the list becomes so long that nothing ever makes it off and you thus never get to check any boxes. In that case, you end up being preoccupied with managing your to-dos.

Your to-do list will then soon turn into a frustration list — the Zeigarnik effect. "It seems to be human nature to finish what we start and, if it is not finished, we experience dissonance", wrote the Russian psychologist Bluma Zeigarnik (1900-1988). As long as we haven't yet completed a task, we continue to walk around with an unsatisfied feeling. In addition, this makes tasks seem like they take much longer than they do and gives you the feeling you are constantly behind on everything.

How can you avoid this effect? Don't use a to-do list.

The
ToDon't
List
Method

The ToDon'tList

Once, a psychologist was invited to the Pentagon to give a workshop to generals on management of time and resources. At the start of the workshop, he asked the group to each write down in 25 words what their strategy had been so far for managing their time and resources.

All generals already hit a wall there, but one: the only female general present. This woman, who had made her way to the top through all the ranks and had also fought in the Iraq war, came up with the following strategy: "First I make a list of priorities: one, two, three, and so on. Then I cross out everything from three downwards."

What the general had done was turn her to-dos into to-don'ts. She placed all her to-dos on a to-don't list and only chose three to-dos to complete. Anything below the line would simply not get done. This gave her more time to do those top 3 things well.

The ToDon'tList method is based on the idea that you can't do everything, but also don't have to. We often think that busy people equal successful people. In order to be 'successful', you would need to do as much as possible. However, those who set out to do many things, ultimately only get a little of everything done. And that always ends up being insufficient.

You are better off choosing a few things you will do well and letting go of the rest. Even if they are good ideas. This decision can grant you some peace, as your brains will cease to continually provide impulses indicating that there still is 'unfinished business' to attend to. Any unsatisfied feelings will disappear.

TIME vs. IDEAS

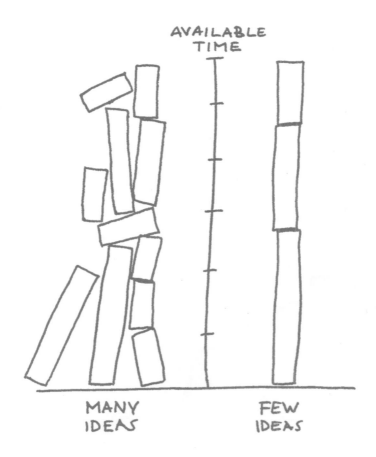

AVAILABLE TIME

MANY IDEAS

FEW IDEAS

Using the ToDon'tList Method

Different levels

What are to-dos exactly? They are small parts of components of an overarching task. Such a task can come from various parts of your life: family, relatives, friends, hobbies, work, research, holidays, etc. (For creatives, their hobbies, work, and private life virtually always overlap.) Those parts can also be subdivided into various components, constantly branching out further — much like a large tree.

It is relatively easy to subdivide your work into various components. You'll have various projects and those projects, in turn, consist of various tasks. And those tasks ultimately consist of to-dos. Those to-dos make up the real work. If you don't complete them, you won't finish your project.

How to add to the ToDon'tList

The more to-dos there are, the more you need to do, and the greater the risk of you not crossing them all off your list. Therefore, it is important to limit the number of to-dos as much as possible.

Assess which to-dos are actually necessary to finish your project. Strike through everything after the third to-do — all of that goes straight to your ToDon'tList. Those are to-dos that you won't be doing right now — and which you therefore don't have to give any further thought.

You can also take decisions on a higher level and put an entire project on the ToDon'tList — including all the to-dos that belong to it. And while you're at it, you could even decide to move the part of your (working) life from which such a project emerged onto the ToDon'tList. Sure, it might be a pity, but you will have more time to focus on the things you are going to do.

TO DO TREE

PRUNING THE TO DO TREE

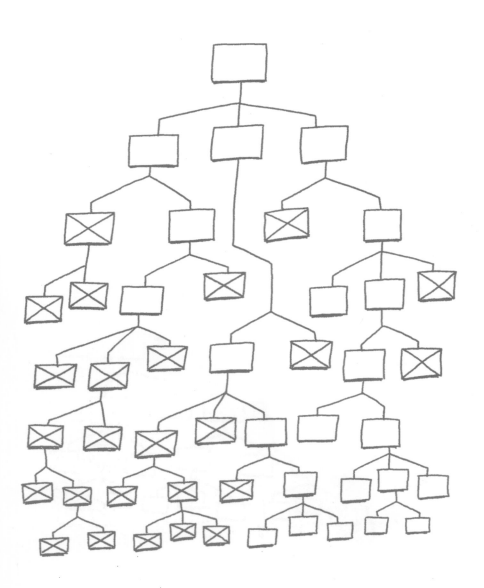

TO DO TREE
PRUNED

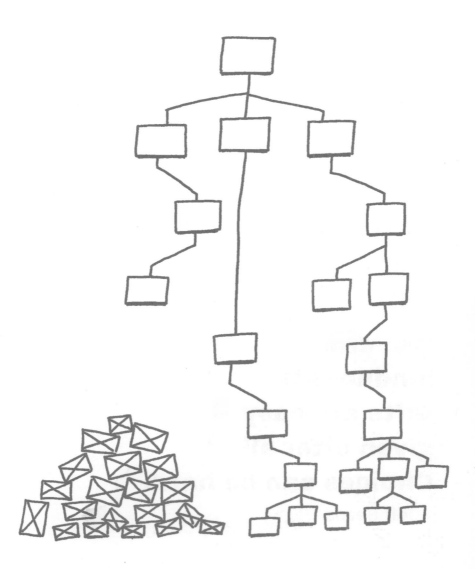

If you go through this process at an even higher level, you will arrive at decisions that could greatly impact your life. Will you take up those studies or not? Will you remain an employee or continue as a freelancer? And as a consequence, will you have enough time left to play with your band? No longer playing in a band also means that you won't have to rehearse and write songs. That might be a shame, but you will have more time to spend on other things.

Making choices teaches you a lot about who you are. If you limit everything you do to 3 things, you will automatically get a clear idea of what you do and don't consider important. That goes for both big decisions in life and smaller choices at a project level.

Choosing is hard, especially if you have multiple talents. Therefore, we will take a deeper dive into the ToDon'tList method in the following chapters. We will be working from the abstract concept of 'Life', through the more concrete level of 'Work', towards the practicalities of doing 'Projects'.

Cleverness is a gift, kindness is a choice. Gifts are easy — they're given after all. Choices can be hard.

— Jeff Bezos

The ToDon'tList isn't just a method; it also is an actual app that helps you make choices. You can find the ToDon'tList app in the App Store. I developed this app together with a programmer friend of mine according to the principles of the ToDon'tList method. Indirectly, the development of this app also led to writing this book.

The app works as follows: You have 3 lists — a Do list, a Done list and a ToDon'tList. You can only put 3 items on your Do list. The rest of your to-dos automatically go on your ToDon'tList. When you've finished a task, the corresponding to-do will be transferred to your Done list (giving a nice sense of accomplishment). This will leave space for a new item on your Do list, which will be added from your ToDon'tList.

Tasks remaining on your ToDon'tList for longer than 3 months automatically disappear, without notification. After all, if they had been important enough, you would have done something about them by that time.

Life:
Make
a Plan

Learning how to think really means learning how to exercise some control over how and what you think. It means being conscious and aware enough to choose what you pay attention to and to choose how you construct meaning from experience. Because if you cannot exercise this kind of choice in adult life, you will be totally hosed.

— David Foster Wallace

The Taxi Experiment

Okay, we'll start off with a thought experiment. You get into a taxi...

→ Taxi Experiment 1

You get into a taxi and don't tell the driver where you want to go. What happens?

Two things could happen. Either you remain where you are, or the taxi driver drives you across the city for the entire night. Every now and again the chauffeur will stop and ask: "Perhaps you would like to be here?" But you cannot determine this. How would you? You have no guidelines on which to base such a decision.

→ Taxi Experiment 2

Once again, you get into a taxi. You give the driver an exact address, including the route you wish him or her to take. What happens?

You will arrive at exactly that address, according to the route you determined in advance. The question you can now ask yourself is: "What has this trip brought me?" If you fix everything beforehand, there is no room for new experiences and insights.

You get into a taxi once more. This time, you provide the taxi driver with some guidelines. For instance: "I would like to go to the eastern part of the city, to a bar where they serve a good daily special and where you can also dance". What happens?

You will now end up in a place you actually want to be, but which you could not have imagined beforehand.

Conclusion: It is good to know the general direction of where you want to go, because otherwise you will never get anywhere. But don't rigidly fix your objective — you want to leave room for new experiences and insights. So make sure you have a goal, but keep an open mind about the road.

You have to have an idea of what you are going to do, but it should be a vague idea.
— Pablo Picasso

SET YOUR GOAL

GOAL TOO WIDE
NO FOCUS

GOAL TOO NARROW
TOO MUCH FOCUS

GOAL WITH
OPPORTUNITIES
FOCUS IN BALANCE

Do What Your Heart Wants

> **If you always do what interests you,**
> **at least one person is pleased.**
> — Katharine Hepburn

Regret what you haven't done

Much research has been conducted into what people regret at the end of their lives. It turns out that people particularly regret the things they didn't do. An American survey even found that 70% of the working population in the US — that's over 108 million people — wake up each day without feeling any passion whatsoever for the work they are about to do. You don't want to be one of them, right?

The ToDon'tList method is all about making choices: choices that allow you to do what you really want. That way, you don't have to regret what you didn't do. Knowing what you want is perhaps one of the hardest, but also one of the most important things in life.

> **It is never too late to be**
> **what you might have been.**
> — George Eliot

The beautiful story of Barbara Beskind

As a child, Barbara Beskind already knew that she wanted to become an inventor. At the respectable age of 91, her dream became a reality and she now has her dream job at IDEO in San Francisco, the company that developed the first mouse for Apple.

Barbara Beskind grew up during the Great Depression. Her first design was a rocking horse. "Well, in the Depression, if you can't buy toys, you make 'em. I was determined I was going to have one, and so I made it with old tires. I learned a lot about gravity, 'cause I fell off so many times." Later on, she wanted to go to Engineering School. Her application was rejected due to her being a woman, and so she decided to study Home Economics instead. Eventually, she joined the army and worked there as an occupational therapist for 44 years.

Everything changed when she watched an episode of 60 Minutes in 2013. The episode featured David Kelley, the founder of IDEO. In the interview he talked about how IDEO is always looking for a diversity of people who can inspire each other. Beskind decided to submit an open application. She worked on her letter for two months — which, incidentally, she managed to reduce from 9 pages to 1. At a senior age, she landed her dream job.

> **It does not matter how slowly you go,**
> **so long as you do not stop.**
> — Confucius

Age is not a barrier

The story of Barbara Beskind demonstrates that we are never too old to start doing what we truly want to do. Instead of regretting that she never became an inventor, Barbara went ahead and made her dream a reality after all. She never lost sight of her goal. There are ample examples of people that did not reach their goal until later in life. Harrison Ford was a carpenter until age 30. Ang Lee was unemployed at age 31 and J.K. Rowling was a single mother on welfare at that same age. So don't lose sight of your goal, no matter what age you are.

> **I am not a product of my circumstances.**
> **I am a product of my decisions.**
> — Stephen Covey

A business that makes
nothing but money
is a poor business.
— Henry Ford

Don't follow the money

People regularly allow themselves to be led by money. Often,
money is their excuse not to do what they really want to do.
But money is a means, not an end in itself. If you truly want to
do what you love, money can never be an excuse not to do it.
Neither is it always a good reason to do something. I have often
worked on projects with the thought "I can earn some good
money with this". Virtually all of these projects have perished,
because there was no soul in them — the primary goal was
making money. Follow your heart, not the money.

How to Know What You Want (What You Really Really Want)

The Taxi Experiment teaches us that if you have no idea where you want to go, you will end up someplace you are not even sure you want to be. Admittedly, knowing where you want to go — approximately — is not easy. You have to dare to be honest with yourself to know what you truly want.

> **Don't limit yourself. Many people limit themselves to what they think they can do. You can go as far as your mind lets you. What you believe, remember, you can achieve.**
> — Mary Kay Ash

Ask yourself this question: "What is something I would be raring to do any day?" Keep your answer in mind while doing the following exercise.

→ Make a list of things you would really like to do.

→ Review the list and be honest. What activities have you added with the thought: "That could also earn me money"? Strike those options and replace them with activities that you hadn't yet dared to write down, due to that little voice inside your head telling you "I couldn't possibly". Don't listen to this voice; add what you want to the list. Including the things that, at first glance, may have nothing to do with work. Simply write down the things that you get excited about.

→ Take your list and pick the 3 things you would like to do most.

There's a chance that your list has surprised you. It probably contains things you might not initially offer up when being asked about your goals. No problem. Let it sink in for a bit.

List of things you would really like to do

The 3 things you would like to do most

1

2

3

DoList

What Are You Best/Worst at?

Creatives usually like to do many different things and can often also do those things relatively well to boot. But if you continue doing all of those things, you will do them at a reasonable level. You will never truly excel at any of them.

What is your Circle of Competence?

It is important to know what you are good at and what you are actually not so good at. Warren Buffett calls this the Circle Of Competence. Everything that falls inside the circle is what you are good at. If you are good at something you also have your heart in, you can truly excel at it.

What does your Circle of Competence look like?

→   Draw a circle. Inside the circle, write down all the things you are good at (skills, positive character traits, hobbies). Write down everything you are bad at outside the circle.

→   Now, strike out all the things you are reasonably good at and the things you are not entirely disastrous at. In other words, strike out the qualities that are not particularly good or bad. Continue doing this until you have a maximum of 3 traits inside the circle, demonstrating what you are exceptionally good at, and no more than 3 outside of the circle, indicating what you are horribly bad at.

→   You have now arrived at your Circle of Competence.

Focus on what you are good at
If you went about the exercise honestly, you will now have a clear overview of where your strengths lie. Focus on those. It is much easier to improve on what you are already good at than to get good at something you don't do very well.

> **Concealed talent brings no reputation.**
> — Desiderius Erasmus

Know the qualities of your 'Dark Side'
The list of things you are bad at is not unimportant. Although weaknesses are not exactly the things you want to advertise all that broadly, they can still be of use to you. What would happen if you started seeing these weaknesses as qualities? Admittedly, they are qualities of your 'Dark Side', but still: things that you are good at from a certain point of view. As long as you know how to apply them in a positive manner.

For example, I am quite impatient. I don't try to become more patient (that's no use), but I do use my tendency to get impatient to my and others' advantage. For instance, my impatience makes me quite good at calling bureaucratic help desks. I simply won't hang up the phone until I get what I want. So, sometimes you can use your bad qualities to acquire good results. Please note: I'm not saying it's okay to be a jerk.

BAD > NORMAL > GOOD > GREAT

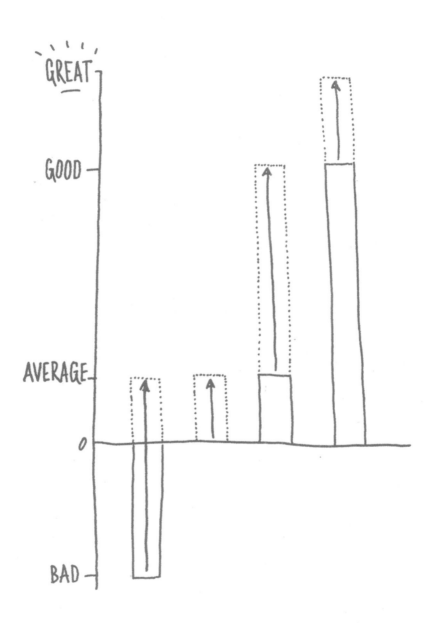

Reveal Who You Could Be

You now have a list of your greatest strengths and your worst weaknesses. And you have a list of what you would most love to do. Great. Let's have a look at what the common thread is. We'll use the overlap method.

→ Draw three circles that each overlap.
→ In each circle you write one of the things you would most love to do.
→ Now it will be interesting to look at what emerges in the parts where two circles overlap. What is the common denominator between the two things that you would most love to do?
→ That leaves the middle part, where all three circles overlap. What is the common denominator of those various things? It's you! Write down your own name in that field.

The total overview reveals who you would be, if you were doing what you most love! The most interesting parts are where the circles overlap. Here, the two items that come together form a unique combination — something that is unique about you!

→ Repeat the exercise using your 3 greatest strengths
→ Compare the results of both excercises; think of ways in which your unique combination of strengths/traits can help you do the things you really want to do.

Of course, you can also do this exercise with your worst traits. That could provide some interesting input, too.

OVERLAPS

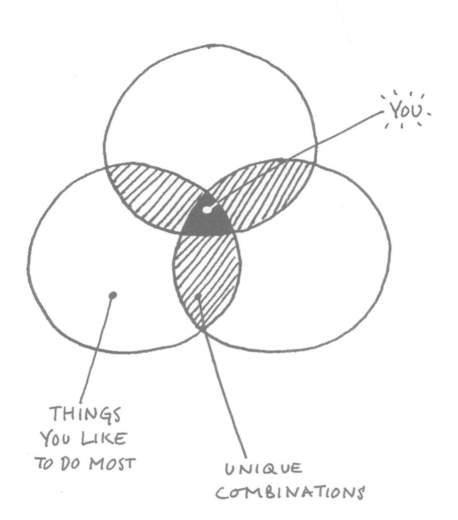

YOU.

THINGS
YOU LIKE
TO DO MOST

UNIQUE
COMBINATIONS

Make a Life Plan in Three Steps

Now it's time to make a plan for reaching your goal. That plan is quite simple: How do I get from A to B?

> **Design is a plan for arranging elements in such a way as best to accomplish a particular purpose.**
> — Charles Eames

1 — Begin at the end

You now know where you want to end up: at what you most love doing and being. This gives you a goal and a direction. Those don't have to be rigidly defined — remember the taxi experiment. However, it is important to know whether you will be turning left, right or going straight ahead at certain points.

> **If one does not know to which port one is sailing, no wind is favourable.**
> — Seneca (55 v. Chr. — 39 n. Chr.)

2 — Where are you now?

During taekwondo training, our trainer once asked us: "In a sparring session, the goal is clear. You want to win. You stand opposite each other on the mat. But how do you determine your strategy in order to reach your goal?"

All black belts immediately responded with: "Closely observe your opponent." Certainly. However, there is something that you need to do before that. One girl with a white belt offered the solution: "Closely observe yourself". And herein lies the crux. You cannot determine your strategy until you know where you stand.

→ Grab a sheet of paper. Place it horizontally in front of you and divide it into three columns.

→ At the top of the right column you write down 'Goals', at the top of the left column 'Where I currently stand'. Leave the middle column blank for now.

→ Write the three things you would most love to do in the right column.

→ Now write where you currently stand in the left column: what you do at the moment.

→ How can you connect the left column to the right column? With the middle column, of course. Head this column with 'Strategy'.

→ Now use the middle column to write down how you get from the left ('Where I currently stand') to the right ('Goals'). What would you need to change in order for you to reach your goals? How can your qualities help with this (or get in the way)? What should and shouldn't you do, what do you need to focus on?

It's as simple as that. If you know where you want to go and where you are now, everything in between is a simple gap-filling exercise. And that will be your plan. But make sure it's not a rigid one. After all, nothing is as volatile as a human being. So save some room for adjusting your course.

Setting intermediate goals can work well for this. Where do you want to be one year from now? You could make a list of goals for each year. Summarise your goals for the coming year in a motto or tag line; that will be your theme. At the end of that year, you can evaluate how you did. Perhaps you will also have done and achieved things that you hadn't anticipated. These unexpected achievements can still be a part of the path that leads towards your long-term goals.

Make a Life Plan in Three Steps

Step 2.
Where I currently stand

Step 3.
Strategy

Start here

Step 1.
Goals

When you know what you want, various doors suddenly open up. That is no luck or coincidence. After all, when you have a clear direction, you will be able to see many more possibilities you would otherwise not have noticed. And you will be better at deciding what opportunities to take and which ones to leave.

I love it when a plan comes together.

— John "Hannibal" Smith, the A-team

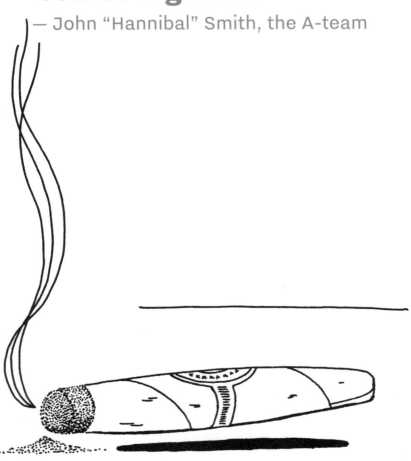

Tell Them What's on Your Menu

Now you know in what direction you wish to be headed. How can you integrate that direction into your everyday practice? It's quite simple: show it. When I was — yet again — working on a new website for myself, I discussed it with a designer friend of mine. I told him that I wanted to do projects that generate an income, but that I also wanted to draw attention to the things I really wanted to do. "Simple," he responded, "I would just put the things I want to do on my website and leave out the other things."

People will come to you for the things you put on your website. And while there's nothing wrong with doing certain kinds of projects for an income, there's just no need to advertise them.

That goes for everyone, whether you have your own business or work for a boss. Whatever you put on your 'menu' is what distinguishes you from others. The fewer items on your menu, the clearer it is what your product range is and the more you can focus on those products or skills.

What's your #Hashtag?

As you probably know, a hashtag provides a message on e.g. Twitter, Instagram or LinkedIn with a subject. You can also apply this principle to yourself in order to help you make choices. Come up with a hashtag that summarises in 1, 2, or perhaps 3 words what you stand for as a creative — or what your studio stands for. It helps you to test whether something you are about to do is in tune with your Life Plan. If an activity or project doesn't suit your hashtag, it might be sensible to move it to your ToDon'tList.

48 **Creating your #Hashtag**

How do you come up with a good hashtag that summarises everything you do? Probably your Life Plan, your Circle of Competence and the overlap exercise can help you think of something. Here are some extra pointers:

→ Imagine someone posts something about your work on social media. What hashtag would you like them to add to it?

→ Is it unique, yet general enough to be understood? For example: a hashtag such as #Design is much too general. There are various kinds of designers, and all of them could use this hashtag. My hashtag is #typeinmotion, because in my role as typographer I mainly design film credits and interfaces.

→ Do the 'Not test'

Create your own visual style... let it be unique for yourself and yet identifiable for others.

— Orson Welles

→ Make a list of all the words that could describe you or your studio. Don't overthink it; write down anything that comes to mind without reservations.

→ Now place the word 'not' before every word on your list. This will look a bit weird, but that is exactly the intention. For instance, if you wrote down the word 'creative', it will now say 'not creative'.

→ Now ask yourself whether there are creative people, studios, or other organizations that would say about themselves: "We are not creative". That chance is quite slim. This means that the hashtag #creative is much too general. Anyone who considers himself or herself in any way creative would be able to use this hashtag. Use this method to get rid of any descriptions on your list that are too general.

#WritingChef would be a good hashtag for someone who loves cooking and writes, in particular cookbooks. After all, there are plenty of creatives that will say that they are not a writer, or not a chef, much less an author of cookbooks. Therefore, this hashtag is unique, but still understandable for everyone.

Now grab your overlap circles again. See what it looks like when you place your hashtag in the middle (instead of your name). Does it fit with the sum of your overlapping qualities? Yes? Then you're on the right path! You have found a good hashtag that can help you assess what you will and will not be working on.

So, what is #Hashta

**Write down your hashtag here.
Oh, and use a big marker!**

your
g?

Create your menu

What kind of project should people call you for? What do they need to remember about your work? The fewer the items, the easier it will be for other people to remember.

→   Make a list of all your skills and projects.
→   Check which skills and projects fit your hashtag.
→   Place these skills and projects on your 'menu'.

You have now drawn up a plan of where you want to go (your goals) and how to get there (using your hashtag and creating your menu). Having this kind of focus is going to save you lots of time. But you can save even more time if you create a routine at work. That's what the next chapter deals with.

When you reduce the number of doors that someone can walk through, more people walk through the one that you want them to walk through.

— Scott Belsky

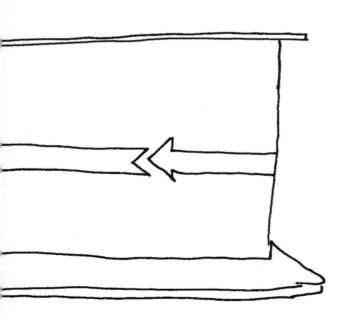

Work:
Create
a Routine

Time is the raw material of creation. Wipe away the magic and myth of creating and all that remains is work: the work of becoming expert through study and practice, the work of finding solutions to problems and problems with those solutions, the work of trial and error, the work of thinking and perfecting, the work of creating.

— Kevin Ashton

[How to Fly a Horse]

Note to the reader: This chapter will mainly be of interest to free-lancers or independent workers. However, whenever a 'client' is mentioned, you can also read 'boss' or 'manager'. Students could in some cases replace 'client' with 'teacher'.

Get on a daily routine...
Working is a process not a product.
— Nicoletta Baumeister

The Dutch writer-journalist Hans den Hartog Jager wrote a
beautiful book on artists' working methods. He interviewed
fourteen of the most important contemporary artists based in
the Netherlands, among whom Constant, Armando, Marlene
Dumas, and Robert Zandvliet. There were great differences in
their methods, but the major thing they had in common was
that they each had a routine: a fixed way of working.

The mind of a creative is a chaotic fusion of ideas and
thoughts. The only way to convert that chaos into work is to
ensure that you organize your daily life. President Obama
wears a blue or grey suit every day; Mark Zückerberg is always
dressed in a hoodie. They both claim to have so many choices
to make on any given day, that they don't also want to choose
their clothes. In short: save time on trivial matters to make
time for those that actually need your focus.

I like routine. It enables me to improvise.
— James Nares

Creativity is being boring (most of the time)

At the end of a meeting for a new project my client asked me:
"And how will you get started on the project? Will you go lie
down on the couch to think about it?" "No," I replied, "I'm going
to get to work." He expected me to find my inspiration by relax-
ing on a couch. Perhaps fuelled by liquor and a snort. I had to
disappoint him: it's not all that bohemian or romantic.

A creative profession is arguably the greatest one there is. But we do pay a price for it: incredible dullness. Creating good work doesn't happen by itself. Even if you have talent, it still is very hard work. No matter how simple or self-evident a final product may seem, — often it contains endless amounts of work, and thus also time.

> **I go to my studio every day. Some days the work comes easily. Other days nothing happens. Yet on the good days the inspiration is only an accumulation of all the other days, the nonproductive ones.**
> — Beverly Pepper

In order to do great work, you will sometimes mercilessly have to say no to other things. So you will have to move many projects to your ToDon'tList and your social life will take on a different shape than that of many other people. However, only working is not healthy either. It is better to regularly take some time off. You can also incorporate this into your routine. You don't have to become a monk in order to be productive. Or rather: be a naughty monk. Don't forget: monks also brew beer.

The quiet people just do their work.

— Joyce Carol Oates

Think of a concept for your studio

In order to create a work routine you need a workplace. Consider your own needs: if you need lots of concentration, you might want a place of your own. If you enjoy collaborating with people, a place in a collective building might be more interesting.

Select a strategic location and consider the setup. Do you often need to print things? Then don't spend your entire day at Starbucks, as you will continuously be going back and forth to the copy shop. And position yourself in the vicinity of your clients. This will save you lots of travel time and makes it easier to run into potential clients and other creatives.

> **I don't really have studios. I wander around people's attics, out in fields, in cellars, anyplace I find that invites me.**
> — Andrew Wyeth

The No Sleep attitude is overrated

Some people think it's cool to 'complain' about how much and how late they work. What they actually mean to say is: 'I have little time for sleep, because I have so much to do and that's because I'm successful.' You could also read: 'I'm so bad at planning and making choices that I am now stuck working through the night.' I feel that the latter is usually true.

There, that is our secret: go to sleep! You will wake, and remember, and understand.
— Robert Browning

Luckily, other people swear by a good night's sleep. If you sleep well, you are much fresher and therefore have a much sharper mind (which helps you to make the the right decisions). Even if you have a deadline, at a certain stage and hour you lose your sharpness. You might think you are progressing, but you're only correcting your own corrections. Go to bed! Get some sleep and get up an hour earlier the next morning. When you're rested, you can do the same work in a fraction of the time. And you'll do it better.

Quit snoozing, take a nap

And then there's the snooze button. Your alarm goes off and you think: "I'll grab an extra 10 minutes". And another 10 minutes, and 10 more to finish. Well, if you have time to snooze for 30 minutes in the first place, you might as well set your alarm for half an hour later. Or just don't snooze and get up! Wakey, wakey, eggs and bakey!

Are you tired during the day? Take a nap! A 10-minute nap will instantly freshen you up. Of course, it is easier to do this when you work from home or are the only one in your studio than when you work from a café or in a larger studio. (That's why my mother used to take a quick nap on the toilet at her work.)

Let's begin by taking a smallish nap or two...
— Winnie the Pooh

SNOOZING vs. NO-SNOOZING

SNOOZING

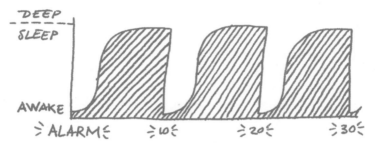

NO SNOOZING

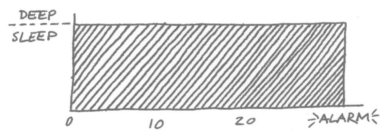

The Joy Of Missing Out

A new age always introduces a new problem. In this age of smartphones and social media that problem is FOMO: the Fear Of Missing Out. Symptoms? You continuously walk around with a smartphone in your hands, or take it from your pocket every two minutes.

Smartphones are mighty handy in various situations — I'm not against them. But they can also make you forget to pay attention to the world around you. That's why I would rather suffer from JOMO: the Joy Of Missing Out.

"Sorry, this is a really important call"... No, it is not

You are talking to someone at a party. Then someone else suddenly gets in between you two and starts a conversation with one of you. Annoying! Why would you let that happen when that third person calls you? You really don't have to pick up. Is that phone call truly more important than the live conversation you were having?

People often say: "I really need to take this." But you really don't. If you first finish your face-to-face conversation and then call back 10 minutes later, the world will most likely not have ended. You don't have to pick up your phone; you choose to pick it up. Whenever you catch yourself thinking "I must take this call", replace it with "I choose to take this call." Then see if this changes anything for you. Of course, you can also apply this principle to other things in your life that you feel you must do.

No wi-fi is a gift

A great advantage of travelling is that you often lack online access. Use the time you are offline to do things you would not usually do if you weren't. Reading a book, for instance. Or simply enjoying the moment without any messages coming in. Whenever I'm abroad, I never purchase data credit. This way, I can't check my email, so I don't have to think about it either.

HIERARCHY OF CONVERSATIONS

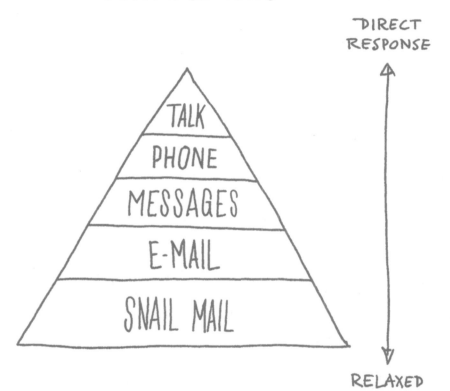

Many people on the road are constantly preoccupied with where they could go online. Once, I was on a flight when the stewardess announced that this flight offered Internet on board. Everyone immediately grabbed their phones and laptops. After forty-five minutes of hassle, I managed to log in. And I found myself wondering what I actually wanted to do online. So that's what I had spent 45 minutes on, instead of reading a book, making sketches or taking a nap. After that, I decided to never again check whether or not a place offers me online access.

Don't bring your camera

During a holiday in Eastern Europe — right before the age of smartphones — I took photos of everything with my snazzy digital camera. And because I insisted on making nice compositions, I needed quite some time to take them.

Halfway through the holiday, my camera was stolen. I lost all my photos, but what a blessing it was, too! I could now walk around and see everything without having to wonder whether I should perhaps take a photo. I cherish many more memories of that part of the holiday. Just like on holidays even longer ago, when I had 36 photos on a roll and could only take 2 or 3 photos per day. We had to be much more selective then, whereas nowadays, our phones are bursting at the seams with photos that often bury the truly important moments.

Social media: The 'Who gives a shit' test

Ah, social media. It is all well and good, but one never really talks about anything much. Just like in the pub. Naturally, that also makes social media (and the pub) such fun. But do keep an eye on how often you visit — just like with the pub.

Should you feel like you're on Facebook, Instagram or Snap-Chat a tad too often, you could get rid of this addiction very quickly. For each post, ask yourself whether it passes the 'Who gives a shit?' test.

→ Read a post and then ask yourself whether making the comment "Who gives a shit?" would be a perfectly reasonable response.

→ How about the following post? And the next one?

→ Test whether this might be the case for 99% of all posts.

→ Close whatever network you're on and start doing something else.

Office Hacks

If ever there was a place you could easily waste your time, the office is surely it. As a creative, you won't be able to avoid office-related activities: administration, presentations, and meetings. And that is not necessarily a bad thing. Colleagues can be inspiring, a presentation can be fun to create, and it is also nice to regularly be able to send out an invoice. However, saving time on office-related activities is always a plus.

Office Hack #1: Email

Let's start off with the biggest time consumer ever: email! If there is one thing people are able to occupy themselves with, it is their email. It is an ideal communication medium, but could you imagine finding the number of emails you receive every day printed on your doormat?

Action = Reaction

The solution for reducing email is simple. Action is reaction. If I hit the ball to the other side of the net, someone will hit it back. The more email you send out, the more you will receive. The problem thus is not always other people's behaviour, but also yours. And it is easier to adjust your own behaviour than that of the others.

If you don't send anything to the other person, that person will not have to answer. And a quick reply doesn't always serve the recipient, either. Perhaps he or she was just happy to get that email off his or her to-do list. A quick reply probably adds a new task to their to-do list.

Isn't calling quicker than writing an email anyway? You should check how long it takes you to write an average-length e-mail.

!! Ignore the exclamation mark

People sometimes forward emails without offering any context of their own: no explanation, no request, nothing. Whenever I receive such an email, I never do anything with it. If they won't take the time to provide the email with any context, I feel I can safely assume that it can't be very important. The same goes for people who don't leave any voicemail. I don't call them back either. And what about those red exclamation marks in emails? If it's really that important, surely they will pick up a phone. After all, you cannot expect anyone to be glued to their computer screen all day.

Five-sentence emails

A well-known statement (not only by Churchill) is: "If I'd had more time, I would have written you a shorter letter." Because people usually don't take enough time to write emails, they often turn into unclear and longwinded monstrosities. Dedicating some attention to your email can eventually save you a heap of time.

The Delete key is on your keyboard for a reason.

— Stephen King

Therefore, should you be planning to write an email, make sure you send out an intentional message, clearly stating what it is that you want. And keep it short. This is actually quite easy if you limit yourself to 5 sentences.

1 — Hi
2 — What you're sending
3 — Need-to-know detail
4 — Call to action
5 — Bye

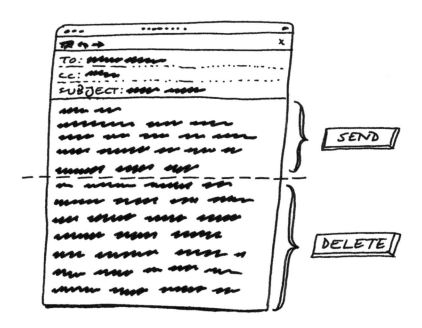

You will then end up with an email resembling this one.

Hi Jane,
I'm sending you the new design that we discussed at the lake.
I've changed the colour scheme to give it a more natural look.
Please let me know whether you like these colours better.
Bye, Tarzan

This way you pose a clear question that can even be answered with just a yes or no. Or even shorter: Cheryl Mills, Chief of Staff at the State Department, was known for only sending a "y" as an affirmative reply, even to Hillary Clinton.

Office Hack #2: Meetings

Meetings are a necessary evil for most creatives. Every once in a while we have to come out of our hiding places and attend a meeting or give a presentation. Meetings can often feel like endless chatter and presentations or pitches cost a lot of energy. Nothing will change that. But you can make the best of it, for instance by making meetings and presentations part of your overall creative process. It is also an opportunity to actively involve other people and the client. If you make use of them in a smart manner, seemingly boring meetings and nerve-wracking presentations can even yield gifts and save you time.

Do your homework

Obviously, it is not helpful to go into a meeting unprepared. Ensure that you know whom you are meeting or who your audience is. (Just Google them if necessary). In addition, ask your client whom they are bringing along and also try and find out what kind of people they are. This will enable you to tailor your meeting accordingly.

Some clients will like you to cut right to the chase, while others will prefer to talk a bit more about the proposal. Every client is different. Some will need you to offer a clear presentation, which can easily be responded to with a yes or a no. Clients who might like to feel more involved in your process should probably be offered various options.

Make it personal

It is more appealing. For instance, if you are a graphic designer presenting a corporate style, consider putting the name of the decision-maker on the business card. And don't be afraid to show your personality. Will your client visit you in your studio? Make their visit to you an experience. For instance, feel free to play your obscure music. Clients will certainly enjoy that if they usually only work in boring offices.

Save travel time with video calls

Face-to-face consultation is necessary, but online communication tools are extremely effective as well. You can look each other in the eye (well sort of) and show proposals through shared screens, without having to travel back and forth. And it gives you the opportunity to work out minor issues, without much hassle.

Please note! Be sure to make appointments with your client. Do not video call them unannounced and also set your own boundaries. I once had a client who would always start Skyping me as soon as I came online. Even late in the evening. I then politely explained to him that I would not always be available to talk shop, even though I was online.

Always check whether you are really needed in a video call. Some people have the tendency to invite anyone even remotely involved in a project for a call. And, as my brother — a lighting architect — says: "Before you know it, you have spent three hours listening to how a toilet bowl is being connected to the sewer."

Be professional, create boundaries

This brings me to my next point: Be clear on which channels you use for communication with clients. Before you know it, you could be using 10 different apps. If clients start sending me important information through Whatsapp, I politely ask them to send me an email. That way, I'm sure I don't lose track of critical information (as I normally only use Whatsapp for gossip, lolcats and beer talk).

If someone calls you while you're on the road, ask him or her to send you their points through email. The main advantage is that I don't feverishly have to go looking for a pen and the client is certain that I have all needed information, as he or she will have emailed it to me themselves.

Office Hack #3: Briefings

You will know your clients by their briefing

The level of your clients can directly be deduced from their briefing, in particular their request and the requirements set. If your client is a professional, he or she will draw up a briefing for you containing all specifications of what exactly their needs are. Nonetheless, you will often encounter questions such as: "What does a photo shoot cost?" or "What does a painting cost?" Naturally, you will not be able to answer these without any specifications. Therefore, make sure that you are clear on what it is that the client wants exactly before you go any further. It is usually quickest to sit down together.

Incidentally, you might encounter overeager clients that create a huge briefing for a really small task (with an even smaller budget). They might even proceed to present that bulky briefing to three creative agencies. This kind of client generally tries to be professional, but isn't. Their way of working usually delays the process. Mainly because they involve themselves in matters they actually have no understanding of.

Do you have a new client who doesn't know what they want? Not even after a long conversation? Then carefully consider whether you really want to do the project. Be warned: it could be a long process filled with frustrations.

Rewrite the briefing

Whether or not the client has made a briefing, it is always sensible to make your own debriefing. You can use this to explain how you interpret the assignment exactly. Don't shy away from spending time on getting it really clear: that time will pay for itself in threefold later down the line. If there are no clear agreements on a project (scope, deadlines, versions, and feedback rounds) it will eventually cost you more time, and annoyance, in the long run.

Ask for the budget

Usually, the client will not want to reveal too much about their budget. Always ask for the (scope of the) budget anyway. Even a little information can help you a lot in coming up with a suitable offer. And because drafting an offer can take quite some time, it would be a waste to spend hours doing so if the price you land on turns out to exceed your client's budget. Does the client really not know anything about the budget yet? Then they will usually first want to inquire into the possible costs of the project. In such a case, you can propose to give a rough price estimate. If the client doesn't turn pale from shock, you can always draw up a nice, more detailed quotation.

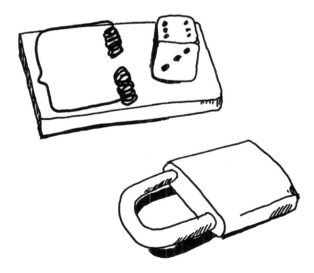

Office Hack #4: Singletasking

With the rise of the Internet and mobile phones, the expectation is — more than ever — that we can carry out various actions at the same time. And of course we can. The only question is: how well?

In this text, tweet, twerk world that you've grown up in, remember that just because you're doing a lot more, doesn't mean you're getting a lot more done.

— Denzel Washington

The myth of multitasking

Whoever does two or more things at the same time, needs to divide their attention. Chewing gum while you walk is not so complicated. Having a phone conversation while you walk will ask for more concentration and will make you less aware of where you're going. But it is still possible to do both at the same time. As soon as you carry out two or more activities that both require conscious thought, things start to go wrong. Try writing an email while making a phone call.

Your memory is full

Your brains are simply not built to multitask. You cannot do two things at the same time with an equal intensity of attention. Really doing things at the same time is not possible anyway. When multitasking, your brain constantly switches between the various tasks. And every time you switch, your brain starts from scratch. The information entering your mind becomes highly fragmented. This causes you to only make half-baked connections in your brain and reduces the chance that the information will eventually end up in your long-term memory to a minimum. So, if you are reading this while calling, you will remember very little about your call, this paragraph, or even both later on.

Missing out

Do you need more reasons not to multitask? If you're always on the phone while walking around the city, you miss out on lots of other input from the world around you. A colleague who makes music once told me: "When I'm travelling, I listen to the sounds around me. I can never put on that 'music' at home." So by not multitasking, you not only create space in your head; you might also be inspired to fill that space with new thoughts and creative ideas.

There is time enough for everything in the course of the day, if you do but one thing at once, but there is not time enough in the year, if you will do two things at a time.

— Philip Stanhope

Become a singletasker

Multitaskers get stressed quicker and start making mistakes. This happens even if you don't notice it at the time and feel like you are being very productive. Research shows that people who multitask have a lower brain capacity than people who are under the influence of marijuana.

People who conduct 1 task at a time eventually turn out to be much more productive. They don't deal with fragmented thoughts and can focus on their work properly. That's why they will eventually finish the project sooner, too. Plus, if you have worked on 1 project for an entire day, you will go to sleep with a much more satisfied and peaceful feeling than when you have spent that day doing a great many brief and small tasks, most of which will be unfinished.

CONCENTRATION vs. TASKS

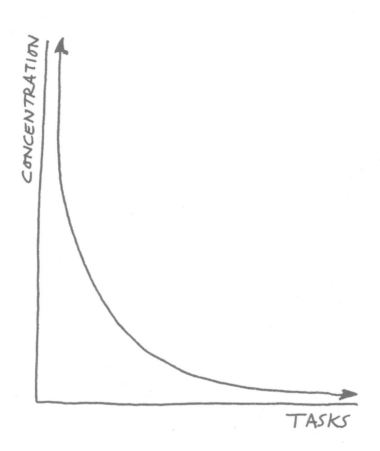

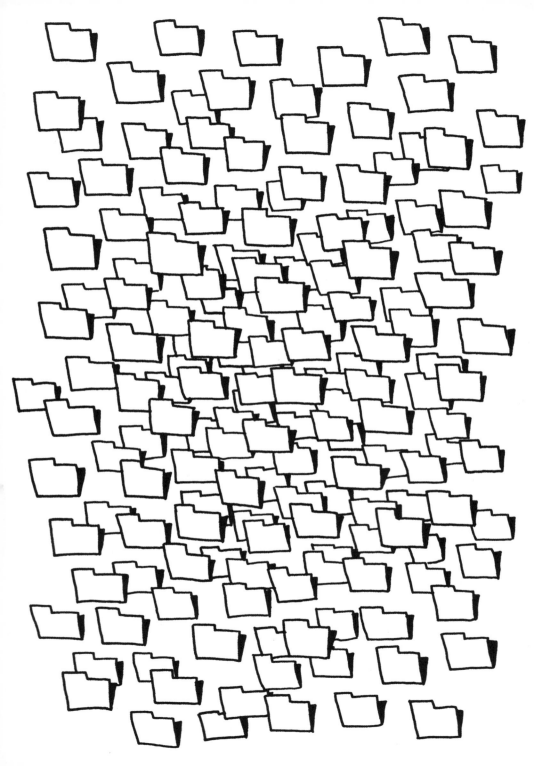

Office Hack #5: Digital Tools 81

Whatever your working method, make sure you organize your work. There are many things that you should not need to think about (or spend time on). Organizing and automating your working method can help you with this. This way, you have more space — physically and mentally — for experimenting.

> **Be regular and orderly in your life, that you may be violent and original in your work.**
> — Clive Barker

Create a workflow
Creative people come in various shapes and sizes, but what they have in common is that they have ideas for creating things. The route they take to get from idea to end result is a process. For this process, you can think of a method. That is your workflow: the route you follow from start to finish.

Create a file structure
Most of us use a computer for the greatest part of the creation process. The great thing about the computer is that it perfectly allows you to organize yourself. However, if you are not careful, you can also create incredible chaos with it. In that case, you will be thankful for the computer's search feature.

You will make your life a lot easier if you start working with a fixed directory structure on your computer. This directory structure is a digital reflection of your workflow. Thus, creating a directory structure also helps you visualize your workflow.

Before you set up a directory structure, ask yourself whether someone else would also understand this structure without you having to explain it to them. That will yield many advantages, especially if other people such as freelancers, team members, or interns will also need to work with it.

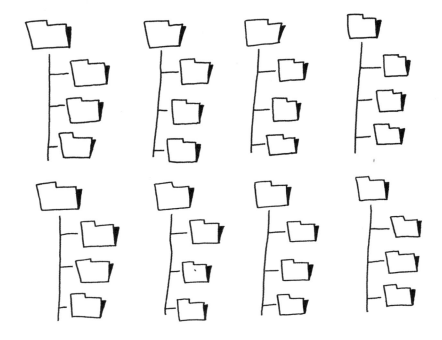

Create an empty directory structure that you can copy and paste for each project. This way, each project will look the same in terms of file structure. It will also save you time whenever you start a new project. And, if you ever need anything from a project a few months down the line, you will know where to find it.

Some practical tips
First, make a basic structure, for instance three folders with the names Current, Old, and Pipeline. Immediately place the

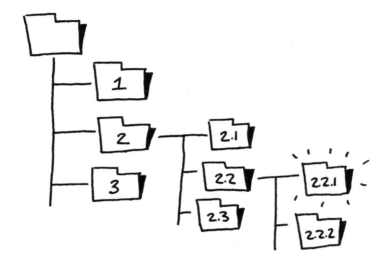

folders that are no longer relevant under 'Old'. You could also base your basic structure on years and/or months.

Working with numbers can save much time, too, if you need to be able to quickly explain where a certain document is located. "The files are saved to folder 2.2.1". Which, for instance, can stand for: 2 Designs / 2.2 Sketches / 2.2.1 Illustrations.

Do you often create various versions of a document? Give your documents fixed names, too, such as card_vs1_commentsAB. This way, you will always be able to find the right version.

Automate everything (that can be automated)
The computer doesn't necessarily make me a better designer. A computer is still nothing more than a digital pencil. But as soon as you know what you want, the computer is a great tool to help you finalize your designs. You can also have computer programmes perform actions that would take hours if you had to do them manually.

You can't do better design with a computer, but you can speed up your work enormously.

— Wim Crouwel

For instance, Photoshop has functionality with which you can automate a certain act. You only have to carry out the technique once yourself, and then it continues automatically. Very useful if you need to edit 10 photos in the same way.

Another everyday example: smart folders in your email programme that immediately sort your email in terms of relevance.

If you know your way around coding a bit, you can even write your own tools for letting the computer do things automatically. If you don't: there is an app, website, or programme for almost anything you wish to automate. A good example is the online tool If This Then That (IFTTT.com). This website allows you to create simple recipes for connecting all your social media channels to each other.

```
fill(None)
stroke(0)
strokeWidth(2)
for i in range(10):
    y = 100 + 50 * i
    line((100, y), (600, y))
```

―――――――――――――――――――――――――――――――――――――――

―――――――――――――――――――――――――――――――――――――――

―――――――――――――――――――――――――――――――――――――――

―――――――――――――――――――――――――――――――――――――――

―――――――――――――――――――――――――――――――――――――――

―――――――――――――――――――――――――――――――――――――――

―――――――――――――――――――――――――――――――――――――――

―――――――――――――――――――――――――――――――――――――――

―――――――――――――――――――――――――――――――――――――――

It might take some time to find the perfect tool. But once you have found the one you need, it will save you lots of time — at least, if you plan on using it more often. If you only apply a tool once or a few times, the search for the ideal automating app might cost you more time than simply doing things by hand.

Online communication tools

There is an extraordinary amount of online tools for daily work activities that can make collaboration and file sharing easier. Always choose a tool that most people in a team have been working with — it is already imbedded in the way they work and they won't have to get used to a new one.

How to select a tool? Consider the needs and the effort the tool requires. Facebook Groups can be handy if everyone is already on Facebook. Whatsapp is convenient if everyone travels a lot, but not so much if you need to share a lot of files. Maybe you need a tool that allows you to assign tasks, rather than only enable communication. In that case, you might be better off with one of the numerous online project management tools.

In any case, do not start by engaging in an endless discussion on what tool will be used. That's a waste of your time. Better to just start collaborating and assessing whether there really is a need for online communication tools as you go.

You are a Pro, so opt for Pro accounts

Many people still seem to have the idea that everything digital should be free. However, digital products are not free just because they're easy to copy. If someone writes lines of code and creates software in doing so, then this has a value. After all, you can use that software to make other things. For instance, a design for a chair. That chair can help people's sitting postures. Therefore, your chair has value. You have dedicated time to your design, which is why you wish to be paid for it, and rightfully so. After all, you are a professional. So why would you not pay for the tools that you used to design it?

Working with illegal software or the free versions that don't have all the features eventually costs you a lot of time because they always only function partially. That is lost time that you can't bill your client for. Check how much money this time costs in terms of your hourly rate to know the price of working with non-professional software. Get the professional version; it will be cheaper in the long run. And it saves you a lot of stress, simply because it works. No hassle, and it makes you look more professional too.

Worried about the expense of a subscription to (online) software? It is not as bad as it seems. An external drive or purchased software used to be much more expensive. Moreover, the online version is continuously updated, which means you always have the latest version.

Man vs. machine

Be careful to only automate those things that distract you from your creative process; not the creative process itself. A computer conducts actions on the basis of lines of code. It is not a human, who with his or her odd mix of emotion, feeling, intuition, memories, expression, etc. can make connections that the computer can never make. That is creativity. Use the computer to grant your brains some space and time for the creative process!

Working Together

Depending on your field of expertise, you will (have to) collab-orate to a greater or lesser degree. Painters and artists often work alone, but also have assistants. Actors and dancers make shows together. Designers and other freelancers work alone, but also in (alternating) teams. Collaborations can be extreme-ly fruitful, offer many results, and save time, but can also lead to endless nagging and many frustrations.

The Right People

If you collaborate with someone, you suddenly have to deal with two creative minds. You no longer just rely on your own ideas; you can also make use of the creativity of the other. However, it is important that you collaborate with people that complement you, that make you better than you are by your-self. The sum should be 1+1=3. Make sure you always work with people that are at your level or, even better, a level higher. That will propel you into an upward spiral. By working together with someone who is able to do something you cannot — or not well — you will create things that would have taken you ages to arrive at by yourself. Make use of each other's strengths and you will make a super team.

Work with complementary people

Although it might seem ideal to work with someone whose work and mindset are equal to yours, this is quite meaningless in practice. Such combinations yield a collaboration of 1+1=2. If you place two similar apples in a basket, you will have a less interesting fruit basket than when you fill it with an apple and a pear.

Teamwork Options

1 + 1 = 3	**Great Teamwork**
1 + 1 = 2	**Meaningless Teamwork**
1 + 1 = 1	**One person is doing all the work Teamwork**
1 + 1 = 0	**Nothing happens Teamwork**
1 + 1 = -1	**Disastrous Teamwork**
1 + 1 = 1 + 1	**Just sitting in the same room Teamwork**

DoList

To Don't List

When all think alike, then no one is thinking.

— Walter Lippmann

A good collaboration is a bit like falling in love. You cannot force it, it needs to emerge organically. The fun thing about falling in love is that you recognise much of yourself in the other. In addition, the other person enriches you with qualities you don't have, without you losing yourself in the process.

The same goes for collaborations. You partly need to see yourself reflected, which will ensure that you will be able to work on something together with the same passion. For the other part, you need to be able to complement each other on a basis of equality. That will make the collaboration greater than the sum of its parts: 1+1=3.

There are two kinds of effective collaborations: between people with the same mindset, who have different but complementary skills. And between people that have (about) the same skills, but have very different yet complementary mindsets.

Note: with 'different mindset' or 'different skills' I do not mean that they are positioned at two extreme sides of the spectrum. I mean that the worlds partly overlap and that parts of those worlds are adjacent to each other.

People with the same mindset who do different things
A classic example of two people working on a common project is offered by teams in the advertising world: 'Art & Copy', or the art director and the copywriter. Together they create a concept for a campaign, after which one focuses on the artwork and the other on the copy.

But very different domains can also come together for collaborations. For instance, as a typographer, I have been making film credits for cinema in collaboration with a visual effects studio for a long time now. Even though each of us comes from another discipline, we find each other in our approach to projects. Together we arrive at a concept, after which I focus on the typography and the design and they work on animation. In doing so, we create something together that we could not have made independently.

People who do the same things with a different mindset
A good collaboration can also consist of 2 individuals who practise the same profession, but work from another perspective. That will allow you to engage in a creative 'battle', as it were. One creates something, the other adds to it, to which the first one in turn responds again. Exactly because you work from different perspectives, you will arrive at an end result that you could not have achieved independently from one another. In this case it is important that you respect each other's work. Recognise the value of the complement added by the other person and add to that in turn.

Beware of unequal collaborations — for instance, if one is subordinate to the other. That creates an imbalanced relationship and leaves you with 1+1=1. Another undesirable situation is when you think you are collaborating, but ultimately do everything separately (1+1=1+1). In such cases, you should look each other in the eye and perhaps put an end to the collaboration.

Working with people on the other side of the spectrum
You will not always have the option of ending a collaboration of your own accord. Sometimes you need to collaborate with people, with whom you do not feel even the slightest shred of connection. Tricky. But instead of sulkily sitting across from each

Working Together Model

	Same Mindset
Doing the Same	Boring
Doing Different Things	Do!

Do!

Um... Why would you?

other, you could also start a conversation. Preferably outside of the work situation. Go for lunch together, grab a beer, or go for a game of squash. That will make it easier to bond.

Look for what you have in common. Even if you are each other's complete opposites, there is one thing you have in common: your joint project. Discover what it would take for both of you to consider the project a success. Then you will at least be in agreement on where you wish to end up.

You will probably also agree on the fact that the collaboration is not ideal. The question that you will now have to answer is: How to get from there to a good end result? Draw up a plan to this end.

First determine your own and your collaborator's strengths and weaknesses, while he or she does the same. Compare those overviews. See where there are similarities and what the differences are. This process will most likely reveal why the collaboration is so difficult. At the same time, it could also give you the opportunity to investigate what qualities can help you both arrive at the desired end result. Focus on that.

And if all this doesn't help... then that leaves you with no other choice than to go to your boss or client and discuss the matter there. Do this the moment you are certain you will not be able to work it out, but before things escalate. In any case, try to enter into that dialogue together. You never know whether and how you might meet again in the future.

Working alone together

Do not get lost in collaborations. Make sure you will always be able to continue independently as soon as the collaboration ends. Nothing is as capricious as a human. Your partner could easily announce one day: "I'm going to do something different." Shit happens.

In other words: never make yourself dependent on a collaboration. Keep following your own path and keep checking whether the collaboration is still part of the route that you

planned for yourself. The easiest method for this is to check at
every turn whether your hashtag still fits with the collaboration.

Does the collaboration no longer suit you? Then go your separate ways. This can be hard, but if you are honest with each
other, you will both know that you might not be the best match
any longer. And if you are relieved, the other will probably be,
too... Ultimately, nobody wants to be in a 1+1=-1 collaboration.

Terminating a collaboration doesn't have to involve a big
argument. Personally, I still maintain friendships with people
with whom I used to work closely. In addition, there are collaborations in many different shapes and sizes. You don't have to
find a joint space from the get-go and share everything. In my
experience, it's better to first collaborate on a project basis and
see where that takes you.

A camel is a horse designed by a committee.
— Sir Alec Issigonis

The Brainstorming Myth

Brainstorming was introduced halfway through the 20th cen-
tury by Alex Osborn, partner at the famous advertising agency
BBDO. Put 10 advertisers in a room and let the ideas flow freely.
This will yield a wealth of ideas in no time. Osborn became
world-famous with his brainstorm technique, which was also
adopted in the regular corporate world. All the way up to the
boardrooms.

For a good brainstorm session two basic agreements are
required: 1 — There is no such thing as a bad idea; 2 — Come up
with as many ideas as possible. In essence, these are perfectly

fine principles. The problem with brainstorm sessions is just that people often expect to find instant solutions.

But it doesn't work that way. In a group, people with the loudest voice will quickly dominate the discussion, whereas the ideas of the quieter people won't be heard. And even though the rule is that there are no bad ideas, people are still careful with what they say, as they are generally afraid of embarrassment. However, the main reason the technique is not effective, is that people in groups are always more afraid of truly innovative ideas. Aaron Levie, founder of Box, once summarised this beautifully in a tweet: "People's reaction to ideas. Bad Ideas: 'That'll never work', Good Ideas: 'That could work', Great Ideas: 'That'll never work'."

In 1958, Yale University was the first to test how productive a brainstorm session actually is. A group of students was divided into two. Both groups had to find a solution to the same problem. Group A had to use the brainstorm principles to do so, while everyone in group B worked on a solution independently. As a result, group A did come up with a high number of solutions, but all of them were middle-of-the-road. Group B's solutions turned out to be much more innovative.

Stay in the box

A common rhetoric employed during brainstorm sessions is that everyone should start thinking out-of-the-box. The problem with 'out-of-the-box' ideas is that a lack of boundaries or limits also makes it impossible to test them. How will you determine whether an idea is good or not?

Think of the taxi experiment at the start of this book. If you say "Just drive me somewhere" you become a leaf in the wind. The same goes for a group of people: if you give them no directions at all, you make them insecure of where to go. Without any preconditions for the brainstorm session, they will come up with an idea, which — in the best-case scenario — people will respond to with: "That could work".

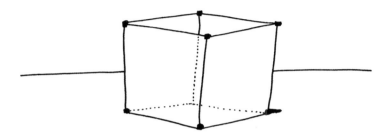

In the book Inside the Box, authors Drew Boyd and Jacob Gold-enberg demonstrate how powerful it can be to actually think inside the box. Find a solution within the given possibilities and preconditions. This will lead you to an idea that can actually be realised.

Artists work best alone. Work alone.

— Steve Wozniak

The thing brainstorming does not account for, is that developing ideas takes time. Ideas emerge in a split second in our minds, but we need time to let them ripen, test them, sharpen them, and improve them. If a musician says that a hit was written in 2 minutes, he or she forgets to mention that the ideas for that song had been cooking in his or her head for weeks beforehand, not to mention that the song is then tweaked endlessly after its initial creation.

After one hour of brainstorming, you might well have gathered 200 ideas but all of those have still only existed for a maximum of one hour and have not yet been thought about much. That's why brainstorming is a fun teambuilding activity, but nothing more than that.

Try Brainhushing
Ultimately, you want to be able to spend the majority of your time on developing and realising your ideas. That is what this book is all about: ensuring that you don't spend time on unimportant matters. Brainstorming is about the opposite: it is focused on keeping the ideation process as short as possible so that you can spend more time dealing with the hassle of the day... But who wants that? So, instead of brainstorming, try brainhushing!

> I used to empty the studio out and throw stuff away. I now don't. There will be a whole series of dead ends that a year or two down the line I'll come back to.
> — Anish Kapoor

You could compare brainhushing to a train ride. You meet your teammates at a station, where everyone takes their own train, but you do agree on what station you will meet at next. There, you meet again and pick the third station together. And so on, until you all arrive at the terminus of the project.

In practice, this works as follows: make sure you have a small team of people with more or less the same thinking and working level. As a starting point, discuss the project for which

PROJECT RAIL ROAD MAP

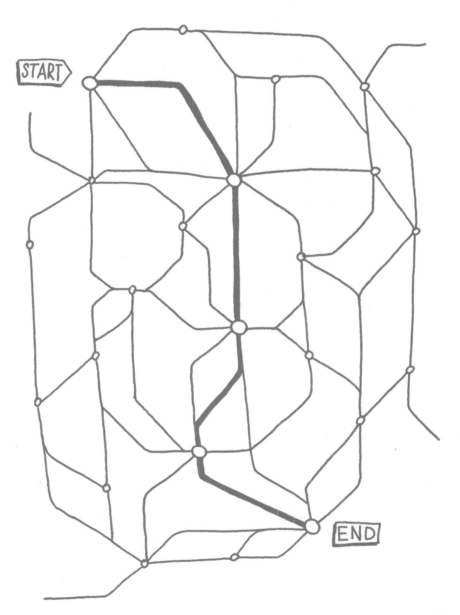

you need new ideas — a few preliminary ideas will automatically emerge during this first discussion. Then agree on when you will get together again. Until you meet at the next 'stop', everyone gets to follow their own route while thinking about their ideas for the project.

When you gather again, let everyone present their ideas and discuss them. Because these ideas have had more time to develop, you will be able to have a more concrete conversation about them. Then, you make some choices (which ideas or basic principles should be used for your project) and continue the process from there.

Subsequently, everyone can think about what has been discussed. This way, you let the ideas ripen in good time. The chance that someone from the team will then suddenly get a brilliant idea the next day — standing in line at the supermarket cash register — is quite significant. This way, you lay down a good foundation for a project. And once the foundation is solid, it is much easier to continue to build on that.

A practical note: It is extremely convenient if the team members are physically in each other's vicinity. That allows team members to quickly drop by each other and briefly discuss components of the project.

BRAIN STORMING

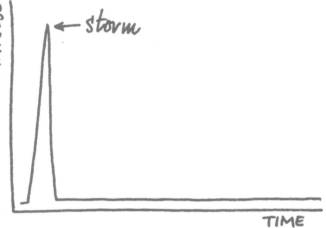

← storm

BRAIN HUSHING

Hushing

A 'no' uttered from the deepest conviction is better than a 'yes' merely uttered to please, or worse, to avoid trouble.

— Mahatma Gandhi

Say No to Coffee Dates (and many other things)

If you're not careful, your entire day will be stuffed with various coffee dates. Somehow people always want to meet up for coffee. But you first need to get there, then you spend an hour and a half chatting, and by the time you get back your lunch break has already arrived. There goes your entire morning.

Why saying 'no' is hard, but necessary

Saying 'no' to someone who wants to meet up with you is hard. It doesn't feel good to reject someone. Moreover, people are often referred to you through an acquaintance, which will make you feel like you have to say 'yes' out of courtesy.

Incidentally, people don't just feel this when it comes to coffee dates. This dynamic comes into play as well when a client or boss requests something you really don't feel like doing. But let's stick to coffee dates for now.

If you look back on all your coffee dates, you will notice that hardly any date actually turned into a fruitful collaboration. That's because people who have a lot of time for coffee dates are usually not very busy. The reason they want to meet — "To see what we might be able to do for each other"— should actually be understood as "Might you have work that I could join in on?" and not as "I have awesome projects, and I feel like I could really use someone like you".

Coffee Date Alternatives

In some cases, it does make sense to meet up. You never know how connections might turn out to be useful or inspiring. Just like those parties that you completely dread beforehand, but go to anyway and which turn out to be the best evenings since ages. You cannot predict these things. That's why you'll find some time-saving alternatives to coffee dates on the next page.

Make it a lunch meeting

When I ran a social media company with a friend, so many people wanted to meet us for coffee that the number of coffee dates got out of hand. So we rigorously put a stop to all coffee dates. If anyone asked for one, our standard answer was 'no', but we did explain why: it costs them and us a lot of time, which we feel we could put to better use.

That's why we offered an alternative: Come and have lunch with us at our office. You have to eat anyway. We combined our lunch break with appointments and we didn't have to go anywhere. If nothing emerged from the date, it had only cost us some sandwiches and a glass of milk (typical Dutch lunch). If something did come from it, it had been an extraordinarily productive lunch.

Drink coffee with a lot of people at the same time

Another alternative to coffee dates is to make a small event out of it. When we were promoting a new digital tool, we invited about 10 people to a nice location. This way we could present our new tool to 10 people at once, instead of having to do the same presentation 10 times. It was also fun for our guests, as they got to meet some new people as well.

Meet at an event you're already going to

A perfect solution for people you don't really feel like meeting in the first place: meet at an event you were going to attend anyway. "Will you also be there? Let's meet up then!" You spend a quick 5 minutes talking to someone during such a gathering, instead of the whole hour it would be if you had scheduled a separate meeting. And if the conversation turns out to be interesting enough, you can still make an appointment for another time.

Don't call us; we'll call you

Should all of the above fail, you could always just explain that you are quite swamped at this moment. Ask them to send an email reminding you of what they want to discuss. This will immediately tell you how serious he or she is. If it all sounds a bit vague, you can simply leave it be. Should you feel that there might be something there, you can reply to suggest a date.

When to say 'yes'
Sometimes it is sensible to say 'yes' to a coffee date. But only if this appointment suits the route you wish to take. For instance, because it is someone you regularly work with. Or wish to work with. Ask yourself the following: If I enter this coffee date into my calendar, will I be able to add my hashtag there? If the answer is 'yes', then schedule the date! If not, offer an alternative.

1

2

3

4

It's Just Work

Now that we have almost reached two thirds of this book, you might have forgotten what all of this is about. We are creative people. We like to make things and think about things. Whether they are paintings, stories, photos, or furniture. This is what we love to do. But don't forget that it's also just work. And work — no matter how much you love it — should not be taken too seriously.

Work?
It's just serious play.
— Saul Bass

Of course, you can work on something very earnestly. But you should enjoy it at the same time. This can sometimes be difficult to manage when you are busy and get stressed. Work doesn't get finished. Clients call about what is taking so long and aren't happy. You start doubting your creativity and yourself. You feel like you continuously need to keep working to get it finished. And then you start doing all the things this book is expressly telling you not to do.

Think to yourself: "It's also just work." The world will not end if you miss your deadline, and nobody will die if it's not perfect. (I missed my deadline for this book twice and you see... you're still reading it).

If it goes wrong, it goes wrong. Accept the situation. Determine what is feasible within the options and time available. Or find another solution, make choices. Leave less relevant matters be. That works much better than putting all your efforts into keeping all your balls in the air. That usually results in doing a little bit of everything but finishing nothing — and that causes stress.

Not everything is for today

Some clients call to ask for something they actually needed yesterday: "Can you drop whatever you're doing and get started now?" You do it, send it and hear nothing back.

Three months later the phone rings again... "We have some adjustments to the proposal you made." That means that you actually had three months to make something you felt pressed to finish as quick as you could. You even cancelled your hot date to be able to work on this... for nothing. You can avoid this by taking the lead when you get such a call and setting a date by which you can deliver. You'll find that the client will usually conform to your deadline.

A request for delivery on Friday afternoon is odd too. The client will only ask for that in order to start the weekend feeling reassured. Do you really think your client needs your work Saturday afternoon while watching football? Ask the client whether they really need it for the weekend. Most of the time Monday morning is early enough.

Keep a top-down overview

If you are more relaxed and flexible, you will see that your clients will respond accordingly. During creative processes things continually change. Especially when you work on something with multiple people. Keep looking at the project on a higher level. That makes it easier to identify what is truly important. If you are too focused on details, you will lose your overview and then every little thing will seem important.

Take your work seriously, but not too seriously. Look for balance. If you just cannot seem to manage that for the moment, then it is what it is. Let it go. Tomorrow is another day. Whatever you do, always make sure you enjoy working on your projects.

OVERVIEW

PROJECT

DETAILS

I go to work every morning with the possibility that I might learn something I don't already know... You should look at every problem and think, 'what can I learn by doing this?' And if you think you can learn nothing, forget about doing it.

— Milton Glaser

Keep on learning, failure is a feature

Doing something you are good at every day will get boring at some stage. You will turn it into a routine task, and that is the opposite of what we want here. Things only remain interesting as long as you continue to develop yourself. That enables you to continue viewing your work with fresh eyes.

The only way to learn is by making mistakes. You make mistakes by seeking out your limits: what is just about possible and what is too much of a stretch. If you make a mistake, you can analyse why you made that mistake and learn how to improve.

That might cost some time, but it also ensures that you bring
yourself to the next level and start working more efficiently.

Perfection is overrated, boring. It's the imperfections — the vulnerabilities, the weaknesses, the human elements — that make us who we are, that make us real, beautiful... necessary.

— Guy Harrison

Perfect is boring

Remind yourself that perfect things are also mind-numbingly boring. It is precisely all those blemishes, those things that are not exactly right, that are interesting. A top model may meet all the requirements set for beauty, but that also makes him or her boring in a certain way. Sometimes, the problem is that there's nothing 'wrong' with something.

While travelling through China, my wife and I were planning to take a fast and comfortable bullet train from one city to another. However, we decided to take a local train instead. It took many more hours to cover the distance, and the seats were very uncomfortable. It was a bit of a sacrifice, but at the same time we experienced so much. You learn and see so much more in a slow local train than you would in a bullet train. You leave the train completely exhausted, but you will have gained 10 new stories.

Quality vs. Delivery

What is more important? Meeting the deadline or ensuring the best possible quality? Both, of course. But sometimes you need to choose. There might not be any time left to achieve the quality you wish to realise. A pity, but it can't be helped: the quality will be acceptable but definitely not your best work. Either that, or you try to stretch the deadline, in which case you will make people wait. You choose.

If I'd had more time, then...

Sometimes a timely delivery is more valuable than a higher quality. If you keep postponing, the process could become endless. It will lose momentum. The relevance will disappear. Ultimately, everyone will start doing other things. And you will still be at it trying to make it absolutely perfect, while there is no longer a need for it.

You will often need to deliver while feeling "If I only had more time, then I would have..." But you don't have that time. Be realistic about the time you have and the result you wish to achieve. There needs to be a balance: so don't make it too difficult for yourself if there is little time available. Perhaps you could create a unique but time-consuming solution for your project. If that time is not available, just don't do it. Delivering a less innovative solution in time is still better than never delivering a brilliant one.

Incidentally, simple solutions are not per definition less good or innovative. It could very well be that, precisely because you have little time and are keeping it simple, you will arrive at a highly innovative solution. More time does not always lead to a better result.

QUALITY vs. DEADLINES

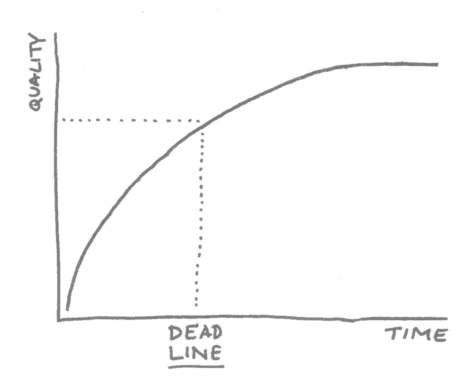

Sometimes It's Just a Job

You will often have good ideas that your client doesn't like. No matter how beautiful or convincing your presentation is, sometimes clients simply won't get on board with your ideas. This could lead to many good ideas ending up somewhere in the depths of your studio or laptop.

You can do one of two things: 1 — Give an even more persuasive presentation, enter into discussions, and possibly hand back (or lose) the project. In that case, it will have cost you a lot of energy without anyone having benefited. Or: 2 — You try to explain your point 1 more time and if the client still won't listen, put your creative ego aside and do what the client wants as fast as possible. Send a juicy invoice. And use the energy and time you have left for your pet projects. In 90% of the cases, I personally go for option 2.

Take the money and run

A teacher at the academy told me that he used to have two agencies. Agency 1 was the one he truly wanted, where he did the projects he personally found interesting. Agency 2 was called NLZV, which stood for the Dutch expression 'Niet Lullen, Zakken Vullen', which means something like 'Shut Up and Make Money'. With NLZV he worked on all the projects that would bring in money. He continued until he had enough well-paying projects under his first agency's name to be able to get rid of NLZV. By the way, no one ever asked for the meaning of the acronym.

Not everything you do has to end up in a design book or museum. Some projects you just take on because they pay the rent. There is nothing wrong with that. Take the money and run!

Projects:
Leave
Out
Extras

You know what you want and you have a plan. The final part of this book will help you approach your projects more efficiently by leaving out as much as possible. It will increase the chance of your project actually taking off.

First, you have to decide which projects you will — and won't — be working on.

The To-Do or To-Don't Checklist
Creatives used to mainly be craftspeople that worked on commission. Nowadays, creatives are increasingly becoming entrepreneurs. They start their own projects instead of waiting for a commission. Those personal projects can form a direct source of income, but they also feature as showcases for potential clients.

Not every creative has entrepreneurial blood. So if you start your own project, make sure that you know what you are getting yourself into. If you don't, you will probably find yourself occupied with things you don't really want to spend time on. Or you might end up doing too many things at once — and nothing ever gets finished.

In order to determine whether or not you will take on a project, answer the questions below. Did you answer 'no' to one of the questions? Then place this project on your ToDon'tList. Even if it might actually be a good idea. And that goes for projects that you initiate yourself as well as initiatives which you are asked to join.

1 — Do you believe in it?

The most important question you always need to ask yourself is whether you really believe in the project. By that I mean to ask 2 questions: 1 — Do you believe that this project has a chance of succeeding? And 2 — Will you be able to work on the project with complete passion? If you earned nothing with this project and nobody ever used it or looked at it — would you still do it? You don't have to think long about your answer; your gut feeling will tell you immediately. If the answer is 'yes', continue on. If it is 'no', you can place the idea on the ToDon'tList before even getting started on the project.

→   Yes: Continue / No: ToDon'tList

2 — Does the project fit your hashtag?

In the first part of the book you defined your own hashtag. A 'label' that you should be able to attach to everything you do. Write down the title of the project and write your hashtag behind it (also see 'What's your Hashtag?', page 47). Do they make sense together? If so, continue.

→ Yes: Continue / No: ToDon'tList

3 — Would you need/use it yourself?

You might believe in your own project, but would you also use it yourself? Depending on what you're planning to make, would you read it, want to see it, touch it, listen to it? If your answer is 'no', why would anyone else want to?

A nice single lady once asked me whether I would like to collaborate on a dating site for creatives. So I asked her: 'Did you realize you wanted that option when using regular dating sites?' To which she indignantly replied: 'I would personally never date through a website!' It would be hard to make that website into a success, I believe. You have to personally believe that something is missing if you want to make a success of filling that gap. Because your experience of the problem also ensures that you know how to solve it.

Of course I'm happy that you are reading this book and I hope that you like it. But I also wrote it for myself. It is something that I would personally like to read. I have read many books and blog posts on creativity and productivity. But none of them helped me to handle having too many ideas and a lack of time for realising them. I make a good living as a designer, but I am not a big shot at a large and well-known advertising agency. Every day I head out to my studio and get to work. That is how I know what one encounters as an independent creative. My reality is what I want to write about and read about, too. So yes, I would read this book!

→ Yes: Continue / No: ToDon'tList

4 — Do you have time to commit to this project?

If you have no time, there is no sense in starting the project. You would only end up with a project that is on your list and on your mind, but not on your schedule. You would never actually get to work on it, leading to feelings of frustration and dissatisfaction. Do you have only a little time to spend on it? Then you will need to ask yourself whether you really want to do that, as your project will most likely get finished much too late and therefore lack momentum.

Do you have enough time to seriously work on this project? Or are you willing to make time by putting other projects on your ToDon'tList?

→   Yes: Continue / No: ToDon'tList

5 — Can you do it yourself?

Would you be able to realise this idea all by yourself ? If so, continue. If not: can you gather people with the necessary skills around you that are ready to dedicate their time to the project with the same degree of passion as you (also see 'Working together', page 89)? Or would you, if need be, have the resources to hire the required knowledge and skills? If the answer is still 'no', what would you be able to change in the idea and project so that you would be able to carry it out yourself?

→   Yes: Continue / No: ToDon'tList

6 — Is there a market (and who is your market)?

This is a tricky question. Of course, you could say that if you personally would use it — even if nobody else would — the project is worth doing. However, creatives ultimately also make things so that other people can see them (or read, listen to, use them etc.). Therefore, in order to be able to really answer this question, it is important to know for whom else, in addition to yourself, you would do this project. And then ask yourself whether those people would actually appreciate what you plan on making.

→   Yes: Continue / No: ToDon'tList

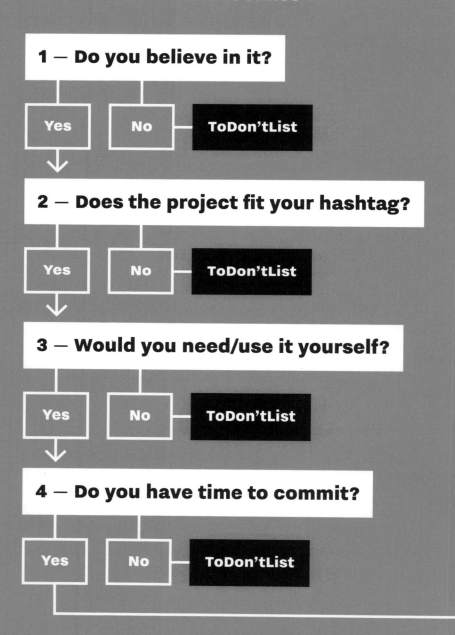

To-Do or To-Don't Checklist

1 — Do you believe in it?

Yes

No — ToDon'tList

2 — Does the project fit your hashtag?

Yes

No — ToDon'tList

3 — Would you need/use it yourself?

Yes

No — ToDon'tList

4 — Do you have time to commit?

Yes

No — ToDon'tList

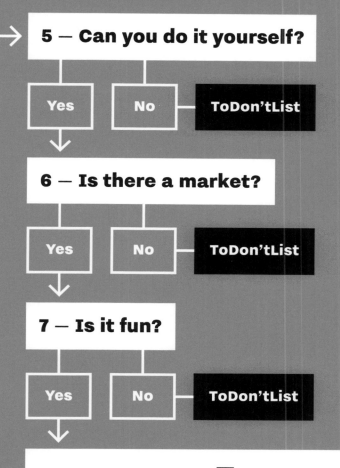

5 — Can you do it yourself?

Yes

No — ToDon'tList

6 — Is there a market?

Yes

No — ToDon'tList

7 — Is it fun?

Yes

No — ToDon'tList

DoList

7 — Is it fun?

The final question is perhaps even more important than the first question: Is it fun? No matter how passionate you are, no matter how perfectly the project fits with your hashtag, no matter how much you personally need it or how great a market there is for it — it also needs to be fun to do. If you cannot enjoy working on something, you will get stuck in a rut very quickly. And when something becomes a rut, it will start costing incredible amounts of energy and time. Better make sure that you find a way of always drawing some sort of pleasure and satisfaction from what you are doing.

→   Yes: Continue / No: ToDon'tList

Just don't give up trying to do what you really want to do. Where there is love and inspiration, I don't think you can go wrong.

— Ella Fitzgerald

The point of no return

A project can meet all the conditions of the to-do or to-don't checklist and still turn out not to be viable. In such a case, you are better off finding out in time — before you have passed the point of no return. That's when you have already put in too much time, energy, and perhaps also money to justify stopping the project. Your only option is to continue, hoping that it might become a success after all.

If it is too late to stop, you need to press on. And when you have got to do something, the fun factor will quickly be exchanged for the stress factor. Therefore, it is always sensible to build in a number of Go/No-Go moments in the development of your idea. Moments at which you can look yourself or each other in the eye and say: "if we stopped now, it would be OK".

Test your project by sharing

The first Go/No-Go moment can take place at the start of your project. Make a simple sketch (or outline) of your idea and test it by pitching it to others. If people understand your idea on the basis of a simple sketch and get excited by it, then you know that you might have something you could develop further.

Ideas are open knowledge.
— Paul Arden

The cynics among us will say that you shouldn't share your ideas because others might take off with them. So what? No idea is 100% yours. Every idea ultimately comes from other previous ideas. However, you are the mother or father of your idea. That means that you have its DNA. If anyone were to take off with your idea, he or she would not be able to take the DNA along with them.

Look at it this way: imagine that someone else walks off with your idea and makes it into a success, while you continue to tinker. Then you might have had a good idea, but apparently not (yet) all the skills to bring it into existence. On top of that: Similar ideas pop up in different places at the same time, all the time. They often seem to float around, they're just in the air.

The most important reason not to work on your ideas behind thick walls and closed doors: How will other people be able to help you? If people know what you are working on, they can also put you in touch with other people that might be helpful. The chance that people have smart feedback or suggestions for your project is many times bigger than the chance they will steal it.

A select group of people that gives you input and provides feedback is something valuable. Their input can be confronting, too, but it can only improve your idea. And it helps you to predict how your project will be received when you actually launch it. This book was also made with lots of feedback and help from others. There is absolutely nothing wrong with that.

Want to quickly pitch something? Social Media offers an excellent platform to do so. Make a sketch or a short text and place it on whichever network fits you best. Ask people whether they understand your idea and what they think of it. That way you can easily collect valuable feedback quickly. If nobody responds, you will also know where you stand.

It's okay to give up
There is a famous scene from Monty Python's Holy Grail in which 2 knights fight each other. The one chops off the other's arm and says: "Now, stand aside, worthy adversary".

— "'Tis but a scratch."

"A scratch? Your arm's off!"

— "No it isn't."

"Well what's that then?"

— "I've had worse."

"You lie!"

— "Come on you pansy!"

And the one-armed knight continues to fight. His right arm also gets chopped off, but instead of surrendering, he starts kicking. Then his legs get cut off, resulting in only a torso with a head left on the ground violently calling out "Come back! I'll bite your legs off!"

If you're not one to give up at the first setback, you possess a valuable character trait. But you don't have to finish everything you start. There is no shame in giving up sometimes. Pressing on when everyone else realises that it isn't working demonstrates less insight than deciding to end something with your head held high. Ending something can also be very liberating. And if you do, you'll take the experience with you — to a next project.

At this point, it might seem like we're doing everything we can to make you move your projects and ideas to the ToDon'tList. And you know what? That's spot on! By subjecting ideas to strict scrutiny, you ensure that you don't get involved in all sorts of projects that are ultimately not viable. What remains is a few really good ideas, which you can then dedicate all your time to.

Visualization Makes Things Clear

You probably spend a long time discussing projects before doing anything about them. Endlessly. Creatives often have a tendency to do so. The danger of so much chatter is that you're never quite certain that everyone is talking about the same thing. We can talk about making something with the 'shape of a square' for days, but as long as we only talk about it, it will remain unclear what exactly the end result will look like. Not very helpful for yourself, and certainly not for the people in your team or your clients. That's why you should make ideas visual as early in the process as possible! Then, at least you'll have something tangible to talk about.

Sketch, Don't Talk!

In order to make something visual, you don't have to do a high-end render or Photoshop impression. There will be time for that later on. Simply start with a few basic sketches. A few simple lines will soon clarify for all parties whether that 'square shape' is a cube, just a square or some other form with right angles.

Sketches aren't made on a computer, but by hand. That is by far the fastest, too. Don't believe me? Let's do the following test. Check the time on your watch. Find your laptop, open it up, start up a drawing programme, select a drawing tool and 'sketch' a square. Now check the time again. How long did this take you? Now grab a sheet of paper and a pencil and see how many squares you can sketch in that same time frame.

Visualize every idea that presents itself to you. As long as ideas reside in your head, they remain loose fragments. As soon as you sketch them, you will immediately see whether they work. And you will often stumble on new ideas; ideas you wouldn't have discovered if you had used your computer to immediately turn your vague idea into a detailed one. Sketching allows you to quickly explore many different directions, which will also lead you to quickly discover the Go's and No-Go's.

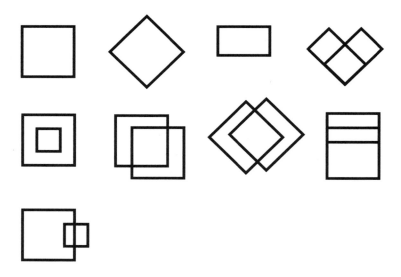

Nothing is more dangerous than an idea when it is the only one you have.

— Emile Chartier

"I can't sketch" — "Oh, yes, you can!"

Do you have a sheet of paper (notebook, A4, back of a letter, napkin, beer mat, the very table you are sitting at, if necessary)? Do you have something to draw with (pen, pencil, lipstick, anything that rubs off colour)? Can you hold it? If necessary with your mouth or feet?

Yes? Three times 'yes'? Then you can sketch. Anyone (even the occasional animal) is able to hold a pencil and draw a line onto a piece of paper. Admittedly, it is easier for some than for others. But we can all manage to jot something down on paper.

Let go of the idea that your sketch should look like those impressive sketches artists make in Moleskine books. A beautiful sketchbook can have a suffocating effect. It instantly puts pressure on you: the sketches you make in the book have to be as perfect as the book itself. And that is absolutely not necessary. All your sketches have to do is roughly reflect the ideas you have in your head. So you don't have to buy an artsy pen or a beautiful sketchbook. Just get a large sheet of paper and a pencil or a thick marker and draw.

Size matters

The thicker the marker, the better. If you use a 0.01 fineliner, you will quickly find yourself making fiddly drawings. They won't be of any use at this point. A thick marker will not allow you to get sidetracked with details that are not yet relevant at this stage. Work big; there is enough time to refine later on.

First Make Something; Then We Can Talk About It

I'll know it when I see it!

Creative: "What kind of creative solution are you looking for?"
Client: "I don't know. You are the creative here."
Creative: "Yes, but it would be very helpful if you could give me some clues on what you have in mind."
Client: "Well, I'll know it when I see it."

You won't be the first creative to have to start a project like this: With a client who wants something, but doesn't know what that is (yet). People need something to say 'yes' or 'no' to. They don't know what they want (or don't want) until they see your briefing — or worse, your finished work. They don't realise that a lot of time has already been invested at that point.

That's why it is important to help your clients define what they want. You can do so by having them make choices. For instance, organize a workshop to help you determine the direction of the project together.

Here's a conversation starter for a client who really has no idea what they want: Draw a square and a circle on a piece of paper — it doesn't have to look good, just draw a square and a circle. Ask your client what shape represents their company's identity best. And then ask them why. This is a way to demonstrate to the client that they, even without having seen the end result, are able to indicate a preference for a direction or form. It's a simple trick, but it allows you to quickly open up the conversation. Subsequently, you could show them two things actually related to the project and discuss which one of those is a better match. And what an alternative could be.

Mood boards will save the day

After you have completed the first basic sketches, the next step is to make a mood board. We used to do so by endlessly ploughing throw magazines, and later on by browsing the internet. Nowadays, you can use Pinterest to quickly create a mood

board. You can make one for your client or in collaboration
with your client. It's a good way to involve your client in the
process, and it greatly limits the chance that he or she rejects
the work you've done for the project at a later stage.

We generally tend to make a mood board reflecting 'what it
should be'. However, it can be surprisingly effective to make a
mood board that reflects 'what it should not be'. That way, you
make both sides of the coin visible, which helps to make sure
everyone is on the same page.

Want to further sharpen your mood boards? This is the way:
→ Choose a project that you will be starting and make two mood
  boards on Pinterest.
→ First consider the mood board about "What it should be". What
  are the similarities between the images? Make a list of those.
→ Do the same for the mood board about "What it should not be".
→ Be critical and see what you can move from the "What it should
  be" board to the "What it should not be" board. Let go of as
  much as possible.
→ Now you have captured the essence.

Conversation Starter

Does the square represent your company's identity better...

↓

Why?

...or is a round shape a better fit for your business?

↓

Why?

Work in circles

When I was still a student in art school, my teacher Petr van Blokland taught us something about design processes that I still apply today. I also regularly share it with my own students at the art academy, where I've been teaching for a while now.

The Linear (Design) Process

Many students (and surprisingly, also professionals) see the creative process as a straight line. We start at A — 'the idea' — and then we proceed to B — 'the end result'. We make something and that is it.

Such a linear process also automatically forms the timeline for the project: Week 1 we are here. Week 2 we get to there, and week 3 marks the finish line. This sounds fairly straightforward and is easy to explain to your teachers or clients.

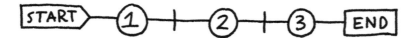

The danger is that you might start thinking: "This week, we will only have to come up with the idea". And "Next week we will focus on developing that idea". After all, that is how it is reflected in the planning. But what if the planning doesn't correspond with reality?

Working on your idea and getting it into focus could take much more time than the duration you scheduled it for. From experience, I know that students endlessly discuss their idea.

By the time the idea finally has a solid basis, the time left for
execution is suddenly extremely limited. Perhaps the execution is exceptionally complex. Or you are dependent on other
people who are not available during that particular period.
Perhaps you simply have too little time. In any case, you are
not going to make it and your carefully thought-out timeline
collapses. And that leaves you with no way out.

Even if the entire process did go according to plan, you would
still have to wait until the end of the process to see the result.
And you won't be able to judge whether or not it works until
that moment. Hopefully you'll find that it works, because you
passed the point of no return early on in the design process.
There is no way back and time has run out.

The linear process may be very straightforward, but it is
also extremely fragile. Once I had a student in my class who
had immediately started working on a huge poster, covering
it with meticulously hand-drawn figures. The idea seemed so
good. But after a week he was only halfway through. And when
he finally finished the work one week too late, it hadn't turned
out the way he had imagined it at all. He had passed the point
of no return the moment he immediately started drawing the
poster. The result: two weeks of lost time and no time left to
make something new.

Start small

What could this student have done instead? The trick is to work in increasingly bigger circles. The way a tree grows. A thick tree didn't grow by first spreading a bunch of roots into the ground and then letting a thick trunk emerge, in order to finally add the branches and leaves. A tree begins as a tiny version of itself, already containing the works: roots, trunk, branches, leaves. The tree is already there, just not as big. But you do have a fair idea of what it will become eventually.

A process that takes you from idea to final product can take 3 weeks, but could just as well take 3 months, 3 days, or 3 years. You could even go through the process in 3 minutes: you sketch a few options, pick one, and 'finalize' it as much as you can in the short time you have left. The end result of such a 3-minute round could be a clear sketch or small mock-up, for instance.

This method requires you to work quickly and roughly, leaving out many details and forcing you to make essential choices. That is why those 3 minutes will tell you a great deal about the overall process: not just what the end product will look like, but also which pitfalls you might encounter along the way. Should the idea turn out not to work or be feasible, then you will only have spent 3 minutes on it, which leaves you plenty of time to start over and try out other possibilities.

Of course, you can apply this principle in different timeframes, going from very short to longer rounds. After the first 3-minute round, you might have a number of sketches. After a round of 3 hours, you could have a sketch model. After 3 days you could have a number of prototypes and after 3 weeks you will have

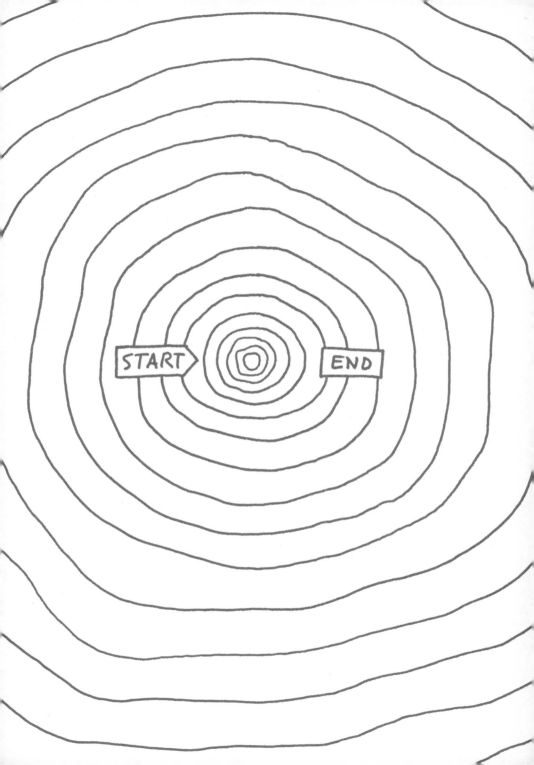

an end result without any stress. The great benefit of working in circles: after those first 3 minutes, you can already discuss the project with your client or teacher. And after a few days, you could have some prototypes to present.

When you work in increasingly bigger circles, as it were, you have much more space to try out and test things. That way you discover what does and what doesn't work. Each following round, you bring your experience from the previous round with you.

The Funnel Model

Of course, you don't have to limit yourself to trying out just one idea. The funnel model can help you try out as many ideas if you like and help you find the best one. It's like a talent contest for your own ideas. You filter your ideas as though using a funnel: You throw a whole bunch in and ultimately arrive at the best idea.

If you distil the entire circular process down to 3 minutes, you can in theory run through the entire process 20 times in the space of one hour. Those rounds will yield both good ideas and lesser ones, but as they'll all be lying in front of you, you will easily see which ones may work and which ones won't. Or you might see that two ideas could actually support each other if you combine them.

For instance, you could select 6 ideas and decide to elaborate on all of them — but this time, over the span of 3 hours. You can then proceed to compare the outcomes and make a selection on which to elaborate even further. Etcetera. Each round you dedicate a bit more time to this process. You will notice that your ideas will start to cross-influence each other, perhaps making it possible to merge them into one concept. Ultimately, you will end up with 1 great idea.

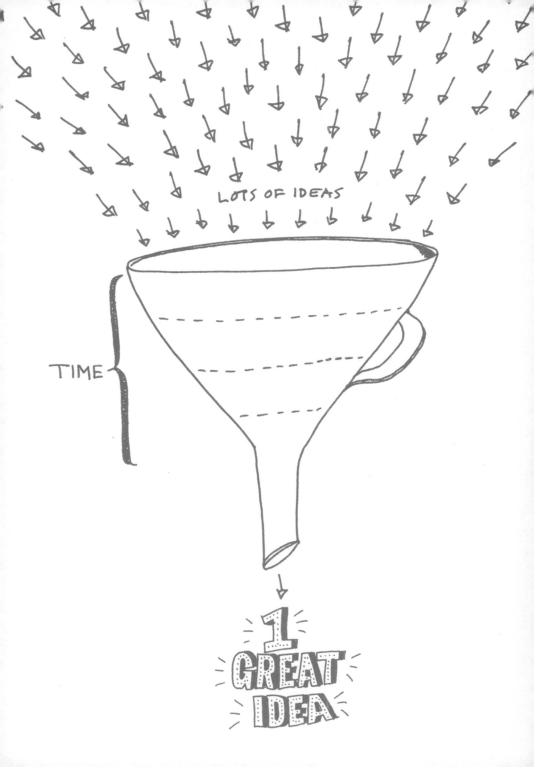

LOTS OF IDEAS

TIME

1
GREAT
IDEA

Start with the obvious

The beauty of bringing the process down to just a few minutes is that it forces you to keep things simple. Perhaps it will make you start out with a pretty obvious solution — but there's nothing wrong with that. As the circles become bigger, you will increasingly be able to make it your own.

Don't try to be original. Just try to be good.
— Paul Rand

It is incredibly suffocating to avoid everything that might be obvious or cliché. If you think that your work instantly has to be unique and original, you put enormous pressure on yourself. Just sketch those clichés that instantly present themselves and at least you will have put them out of your mind for the time being. And who knows where they will take you.

No Add-ons, But Leave-outs

If you have ever organized a party, you know how complicated just making the guest list can get: We really should invite weird aunt Agatha, but if we do, then we also need to invite annoying uncle Fritz with his stupid jokes. And if we invite him, it would just be rude not to invite binge-drinking Gerald and Petunia.

Before you know it, your party is full of people you don't even really like. The solution is obvious: If you don't invite aunt Agatha, you are instantly relieved of all those other people too.

Remove Complexity

When we create something, we quickly tend to add a variety of things. If we do this, then we really should add this, too. And that! But anything you add immediately brings a whole set of questions to consider. And these will sooner or later also end up on your to-do list. The less you add, the less extra work you will have to do.

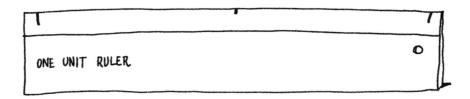

ONE UNIT RULER

Less = Less

The more you add, the more links there are to the chain. The more links you have, the bigger the chance that one breaks and ruins the entire thing. Or, in other terms: It is harder to juggle 10 balls than 2.

The more you leave out, the easier it becomes to launch a project. For instance, our ToDon'tList app was relatively easy to realize because we left out as many features as possible. This principle also applies to other factors like team size. It costs more effort to keep every member of a big team productive because such a team contains more links, more opinions and therefore more hassle. This is why large companies are often so bureaucratic. A better approach is to get your project up and running by yourself (or with a small team) first. You can always decide to upsize it later.

What's the most basic version?

Always ask yourself what the simplest version is of what you want to make or do. What is the leanest version of the product? Make a list of everything you would want the product to do or contain. Then choose three things that are truly necessary. This might be hard to do (let mood boards help you), but this is the way to get to the essence of your product. Then, work on those necessary aspects and put the rest on your ToDon'tList for the time being.

Here we see the recurrence of the question: will you go for quality or delivery? (See also page 114.) You can endlessly work on reaching the most complete version and then test what the world thinks of it. But you can also launch the most basic version and fine-tune and complement that version based on experience and feedback. Perhaps the feedback you receive will point you into an entirely different direction — one that you could not have anticipated if you had not launched the product at an early stage.

Give yourself some rules

You can also choose to give yourself a set of rules, within which you need to find a solution. Such self-imposed limits force you to make choices and allow you to approach the options you have much more creatively.

If you set rules for yourself, you will no longer have to consider a number of questions. Imagine you have set the rule that the only colour you will be using is red. Then you no longer

need to think about colour. Or what material to use, or which
tools. You don't only save yourself time, but you also challenge
yourself to find new possibilities within the limits of your own
rules.

Matthew Herbert is a well-known British DJ and producer.
He is known for his experimental electronic music, for which
he mainly samples the sounds of objects. His website lists what
materials he uses for each tune: "71 copies of The Sun newspa-
per, 1 McDonald's filet o'fish, 1 person being cremated, a dozen
organic eggs from Tesco's, a club full of people kissing'. Herbert once explained in an interview that you can make any
sound you want when you have a studio with comprehensive
electronic equipment — but that it gets more interesting if you
decide to not use that equipment. Then you have to go and look
for other possibilities to get the sound you want.

I can make music out of a banana or David Cameron or Belgium.
— Matthew Herbert

Be an anarchist
When there are rules, even if they are your own, you can of
course break them.

For a while, I was part of a cooking club that set a different
limitation for each cooking session. For instance, all courses
must be yellow. Or, cook a three-course meal for €3 per person.
If you need to cook three courses for €3, you could look for the
cheapest products. But you could also grow them yourself.

A few vegetable seeds cost virtually nothing. And there was no rule specifying that you could not grow your own food. My point: go and look for the loopholes.

When I started writing this book, one of my rules was: no quotes by Steve Jobs. Of course, a book like this calls for quotes from the Apple founder. But by expressly avoiding those, you end up discovering other people with interesting ideas. Still, I have included 1 quote by co-founder Steve Wozniak (page 99), as there was no rule about other Apple people — and I enjoyed naming the man in Steve Jobs' shadow for once.

Kill Your Darlings

In theory it all sounds simple enough, but leaving out as much as possible is not always that easy in practice.

There is no such thing as simple. Simple is hard.
— Martin Scorsese

When I finished the first version of this book, it consisted of more than 45,000 words. However, the agreement with the publisher had been that the book would contain 22,000 words. That meant that more than half of all my writing had to go. On the basis of feedback, I started removing all the sections that were not directly linked to time management. To be fair, I might never have done so if there hadn't been a word limit. That limit very possibly saved the book (and otherwise my wife did, as she edited the book splendidly).

I try to leave out the parts that people skip.

— Elmore Leonard

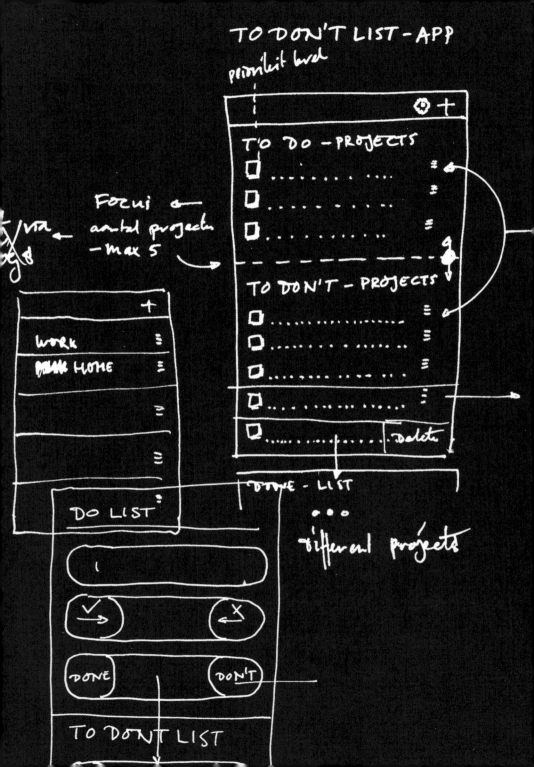

The ToDon'tList App

As mentioned before (page 23), a programmer friend and I made a ToDon'tList app, an app that helps you make choices and keep track of your goals. We created it according to the ToDon'tList method before we even called it a method.

Making of

The ToDon'tList became a household term in the studio when I ran a social media company with a friend. It was something we'd often say: "Good idea, but we'll just park it on the To-Don'tList for now." The very idea to make a ToDon'tList app also spent some time on the ToDon'tList.

That is, until I met Frank, with whom I collaborated on an entirely different app at the time. Frank was excited and said that if I could keep the app as simple as possible, he would be willing to programme it — a great example of collaboration between two people from different disciplines, but with the same passion for a project.

In order to keep the app simple, we came up with the following restrictions:

→   No more than one list

One list prevents people from creating heaps of lists again, which they will eventually stop managing, because it costs them too much time. Users can personally choose at what level they wish to use the list. Frank uses the app for programming. I use it to organize my ideas for new projects.

→   No extra sub-features

The app is just a list. You can't add any tags to your items, you can't share anything, and you can't post to social media. The app has one button: for adding something to your ToDon'tList. From there you decide whether you move this new item to your DoList.

→ Only black, white and one highlight colour

No extra colours. Black, white and one highlight colour are enough to shape the app. That also applied to the design of this book. One rule that applies to me as a typographer is that I generally only work with fonts from font designers I know personally. In this case, those are the Nitti Grotesk by Pieter van Rosmalen and the Mala by Barbara Bigosińska.

Why is there no Android version yet? Let's first see whether iPhone users like the app. If they do, we can think about an Android version. For now, it's still on the ToDon'tList.

#ToDontList

In Conclusion

References

I didn't think of everything in this book by myself. My ideas evolved from other ideas, all of which I consider to be open knowledge. So feel free to use them, too.

I got my inspiration from other creatives I collaborated with. From teachers and mentors. At conferences. From documentaries. I found them in books or blog posts that I've read recently or long ago. I even read the term ToDon'tList once in a blog. Unfortunately, I was never able to find that blog post again. Many of the quotes were found online. That also means that I can't be absolutely certain they actually came from the people they are accredited to — which does not negate their intrinsic value.

Wherever possible, I have referenced the sources directly in the text. Seeing as a thorough investigation into the source of every detail would be an extremely labour-intensive task, I have placed that on my ToDon'tList for now. Should there be a source or reference that in your opinion has not been mentioned (correctly), I would love to hear from you. The source will then be included in a following edition.

Word of thanks

Of course, I didn't write this book completely by myself either. My brother Benz Roos was the first to make his way through the first draft and helped me separate the sense from the nonsense.

My wife Anne de Bruijn did an amazing job editing/co-writing the entire book, making it into a readable story. In addition, she ensured that during the writing process I kept coming back to what it's all about: our beautiful son Oswald, who was born during the making of this book. At the age of three months, Oswald taught me that multitasking really doesn't work: "You either have your laptop on your lap or me, not both of us."

Frank van der Peet wrote all the lines of code for the To-Don'tList app. Moreover, he made sharp contributions to the concept. Whenever I came up with a new idea, his standard reply was: "Great idea, but it doesn't fit in with the principles of the ToDon'tList."

Finally, thanks to Peter Heykamp who encouraged me to pour all my ideas on time management into a book. He introduced me to the wonderful people at BIS Publishers. Peter kept me on my toes in his role as art director and sounding board. And each time I had put the ToDon'tList project on my own To-Don'tList because I was too busy with other things, he ensured that I placed the project back onto my DoList again.

Thank you all for your time!
Donald

Table of Contents

Why Creative People Need Time Management — 6
Where Do Ideas Come From? — 10
The To-Do List — 12

The ToDon'tList Method — 14
The ToDon'tList — 15
Using the ToDon'tList Method — 18

Life: Make a Plan — 24
Choose a Direction, Set a Goal — 27
Do What Your Heart Wants — 30
How to Know What You Want
(What You Really Really Want) — 33
What Are You Best/Worst at? — 36
Reveal Who You Could Be — 40
Make a Life Plan in Three Steps — 42
Tell Them What's on Your Menu — 47

Work: Create a Routine — 54
Daily Routine — 57
Go to Bed! — 61
The Joy Of Missing Out — 64
Office hacks — 68
    Office Hack #1: Email — 69
    Office Hack #2: Meetings — 72
    Office Hack #3: Briefings — 74
    Office Hack #4: Singletasking — 76
    Office Hack #5: Digital Tools — 81
Working Together — 89
    The Right People — 89
    The Brainstorming Myth — 97
Say No to Coffee Dates (and many other things) — 105
    Coffee Date Alternatives — 105
    Quality vs. Delivery — 114
    Sometimes It's Just a Job — 116

Projects: Leave Out Extras — **118**

The To-Do or To-Don't Checklist — 121
Go/No-Go — 127
Visualization Makes Things Clear — 131
    Sketch, Don't Talk! — 131
    First Make Something; Then We Can Talk About It — 136
Work in circles — 140
    The Linear (Design) Process — 140
    The Circular (Design) Process — 142
No Add-ons, But Leave-outs — 147
    Remove Complexity — 147
    Give yourself some rules — 148
    Kill Your Darlings — 150

The ToDon'tList App — 153

In Conclusion — 156

Creative Credits
Written, designed & illustrated* by Donald Roos
Co-written & edited by Anne de Bruijn
Art direction by Peter Heykamp
App development by Frank van der Peet

*Illustrations straight from Donald's sketchbooks.
Donald posts sketches on Instagram and Twitter regularly. Follow @Bureaudonald
Photo cover by Dennis Wielaert

BIS Publishers
Building Het Sieraad
Postjesweg 1
1057 DT Amsterdam
The Netherlands
T +31 (0)20 515 02 30
bis@bispublishers.com
www.bispublishers.com

ISBN 978-90-6369-423-4

→   Any suggestions, questions or requests for workshops?
     Please send a 5 sentence email to donald@todontlist.net